• World Famous •

SPORTING MOMENTS

. *World Famous* .

SPORTING
MOMENTS

Mark Daniel

MAGPIE
London

Magpie Books Ltd
7 Kensington Church Court
London W8 4SP

First published in the UK 1994
Copyright © Magpie Books Ltd
Illustrations and cover pictures © Popperfoto
and Bob Thomas Sport Photography

ISBN 1 85813 384 X

Typeset by Hewer Text Composition Services, Edinburgh
Printed in Finland by
Werner Söderström Oy

Contents

Chapter one: **Classic Confrontations**   1
Horizontal Heavyweights, "Our 'Enery" and Cassius Clay   2
Fangio and Hawthorn   6
The World Cup, 1966   8

Chapter two: **Scandals**   13
"The Hand of God"   14
An Exhibition   15
Those Pernicious Full Marks   17

Chapter three: **Upsets**   21
Snooker: The 1985 World Championship   22
A One-Off   26
The All Blacks   28

Chapter four: **Mishaps and Disasters**   33
Devon Loch   34
Le Mans, 1955   36
Sensational Nationals   38

Chapter five: **Comebacks**   43
22–24   44
"Humpty"   45
Celtic v Inter Milan, 1967   48
Jessop's Test, 1902   51
Nigel Mansell   53
The Greatest Collapse – the Greatest Recovery!   55

Chapter six: **Staying Power**   59
Liverpool in Europe   60
Desert Orchid   64
Ten Seconds   66

Chapter seven: **Records**   69
Jesse Owens   70
Jack Hobbs   71
Roger Bannister's Four Minute Mile   74
Laker, Lock and Shackleton – the Year of the Bowlers   75
Bob Beamon's Flight   78
Mark Spitz's Seven Golds   79

Chapter eight: **The Greatest Ever**   83
Arkle: Death and Disaster at Kempton Park   84
Two Immortal Tries   87
Pedal Prestidigitation   90
Grundy and Bustino   93
The Gareth Edwards Try   96
The Great White Shark   97

The Real All-Rounders   101

• chapter one •

CLASSIC
CONFRONTATIONS

Horizontal Heavyweights, "Our 'Enery" and Cassius Clay

It is a sad fact that British heavyweight boxers . . . well, are no damned good. Except for the legendary Bob Fitzsimmons (who had emigrated to New Zealand at nine), no British boxer has won a heavyweight title bout against an American opponent. So dire is the British record that a 1920s sports journalist dubbed the British challengers "the Horizontal Heavyweights".

Notable amongst British champions was Phil Scott, who ruled the British ring from 1926 to 1931. Against American opposition, his technique was to clutch his nether regions and sink to the canvas with a faint but distinctly audible gasp of "Foul!" He was nicknamed "Phainting Phil" by the American press.

Amazingly, he won on disqualification many times, against George Cook, Armand de Coratis, Ricardo Bertazollo, Ted Sandwina, Otto Van Porat and others. The great Jack Dempsey refereed the Van Porat fight. He begged the prostrate Englishman to continue, but Scott stayed down.

Dempsey had to disqualify Van Porat, but not before delivering a scathing summation of Phainting Phil's stratagem. In the end, Phainting Phil got his come-uppance. His opponent, Jack Sharkey, almost certainly *did* hit Scott low, but nobody cared. The referee, to American cheers, simply counted him out.

Notwithstanding his method, Phil Scott may well have been Britain's most successful ever heavyweight against American opposition. Otherwise, Britain has specialised in heavyweight fighters with endearingly goofy grins whom everyone in Britain loves and nobody fears.

Jack Bloomfield was a promising heavyweight contender. In 1922, he showed just how promising when he fought former British champion Bombardier Billy Wells (once charmingly described by a prospective opponent as "all chin from the waist up"). Bloomfield knocked Wells out. After the statutory count, he tried to lift the unconscious man to drag him back to his corner, and suffered a hernia which ended his boxing career.

Amateur welterweight Rich Keeling was able to knock out Bill Redford in 1952, but found himself outclassed a moment after the count. Redford's enraged mother jumped into the ring and laid him out with one right haymaker.

The exception to this rule was Henry Cooper. The British public did their best to turn him into a harmless "boy next door". They referred to him as "Our 'Enery", and he, by nature an amiable sort, played up to them. He lacked, perhaps, the true killer instinct of the great champions and, of course, his eyes, ever susceptible to cuts, let him down. Nonetheless, he was a fighter, and able, on one memorable occasion, to trouble America's greatest boxing export.

In June, 1963, Cassius Clay was well on his way to becoming the most famous man on earth. His physical beauty, his astonishing speed, his taunting, dancing style, more commonly associated with the lower weights, and his extraordinary gift for self-promotion had made him renowned, sometimes reviled, always respected, throughout the world.

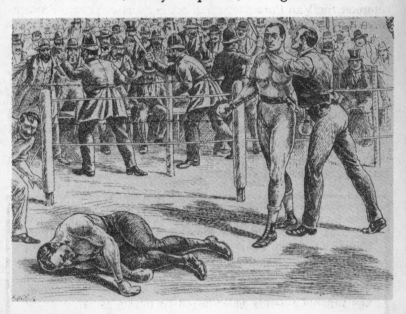

Bob Fitzsimmons beat Jack Dempsey (1891).

Clay had turned professional at the end of 1960, after picking up the light-heavyweight gold at the Rome Olympics. He had modelled his provocative boasting and flaunting on a wrestler named "Georgeous George", who packed stadia in the States.

George never entered the ring until his valet, in morning-dress, had fumigated the ring – and George's opponent – with a Flit gun of scented disinfectant. George then made his appearance in a fur-trimmed robe. With his blond hair in a hairnet, he then insulted old ladies and provoked hecklers and, between rounds, combed his hair before a mirror held by his valet.

Clay did not go quite so far, but he had learned from George that punters loved nothing so much as a cocky champion and the prospect of his getting a thrashing. He took to predicting his victories, usually in verse. On this occasion, of Cooper, he predicted, "If he wants to jive, he'll fall in five."

After two good fighting rounds, Clay's right hand hit Cooper's left eyebrow and the old trouble began. With a cut of over two inches in length and blood trickling down over his eye, it could only be a matter of time before the fight was stopped. He went on the offensive. With a series of jabs, he forced Clay back against the ropes. The dancing had stopped. Cooper's finest blow, his left hook, smashed into Clay's jaw. True, he might never have hit Clay had it not been for the ropes, but the ropes absorbed some of the weight of the blow and slowed the champion's fall. There was a count of five. The bell rang.

There was some clever gamesmanship now. Clay's trainer, Angelo Dundee, noticed a tiny rip in Clay's glove. He inserted his finger to test its extent, making the tear even worse. He called to the referee. By the time that a new pair of gloves had been found, the inter-round interval of one minute had been extended to two. Clay's clouded head had cleared.

In the fifth, Clay attacked that injured eye. It was only minutes before Cooper's manager threw in the towel.

The longest fight with bare knuckles took place in Melbourne, Australia, between Jas. Kelly and Jonathan Smith in November, 1855. It lasted six hours and 15 minutes. The longest glove fight was between A. Bowen and J. Burke in New Orleans on April 6, 1893. It went 110 rounds, lasting seven hours and 19 minutes. After all that, it ended in a draw.

Former world heavyweight champion Max Baer had a heart attack in a New York hotel. He managed to stagger to the telephone and call reception. "Get me a doctor," he gasped. The receptionist told him that the house doctor was on his way. "No, dummy," said Baer, "I want a *people* doctor."

Nearly three years later, Cooper faced Clay – now Muhammad Ali and World Champion – again. Cooper fought well, but again his eyes let him down and the fight was stopped.

Twice defeated by perhaps the greatest fighter of all time, without once hitting the canvas, "Our 'Enery" had done much to make up for the dishonour of "Phainting Phil".

Ali, as a Black Moslem, was a conscientious objector to the Vietnam War and refused to respond to the draft. In (admittedly curious) consequence, he was stripped of his world title.

The championship was put up for grabs. Eight heavyweights were named as contenders. One of them was Joe Frazier. Frazier refused to take part. The other nominated fighters went through a painful and essentially unsatisfactory knock-out series of fights. Jimmy Ellis ended up as nominal Champion of the World. Frazier challenged him – and stopped him in five rounds.

Now, one year later, Ali was back, and hungry for his title. It was a classic sporting confrontation, not least because of the differences between the two men. Smokin' Joe was a deep-South boy, an in-fighter, four inches shorter than Ali. He did not talk much. No one ever accused Ali of taciturnity.

There had been those who had accused Ali of having a "glass jaw", largely in hope rather than from empirical observation. The fact was that Ali had been hit so little that no one knew how well he could withstand an onslaught.

We learned that night in Madison Square Gardens.

It was a fierce, no holds barred contest. Ali wanted his title back. He had taunted Smokin' Joe, but Smokin' Joe was a tough, fiercely proud man who was not going to yield to any jumped up liberal who mocked him as an "Uncle Tom".

Ali's old skill had not deserted him, and, in the early rounds, his constant, gadfly jabbing took its toll. But Ali had been three years off-work. He tired quickly. Soon, he was using the ropes. So was Frazier. He worked his way in there. He attacked Ali's body with a ferocious onslaught of hooks and jabs and upper-

England captain Bobby Moore holds aloft the World Cup Trophy, 1966.

cuts. In the eleventh, he had Ali down, though Ali, and the referee, preferred to call it a slip.

Ali's glass jaw was proved a myth. He fought back. In the fourteenth, the punishment on both sides was terrible and wonderful. In the fifteenth, a perfect Frazier left hook left Ali flat on his back, blinking up at the arc-lights. He took the "eight". He came back. The bell ended a tussle such as few of us have seen, before or since. Frazier won on points. Frazier, it has to be said, deserved to win on points. But for once it had been a fight between deserving champions, not champions set against Aunt Sallys.

Fangio and Hawthorn

Those who were there speak of it with awe: an in-fighting, nigh hand-to-hand duel at 120 mph. The date was 5 July, 1953. The place was Reims. The event, the French Grand Prix.

Juan Manuel Fangio, the greatest racing driver of his generation, led the Maserati team. At that time, Maseratis were perhaps the most powerful racing-cars in the world. Ranked alongside Fangio in the Maserati team were Felice Bonetto, Pinocho Marimon and Froilon Gonzalez.

Maserati had the power, but Enzo Ferrari's cars were more manoeuvrable, quicker to respond. His team consisted of Giuseppe Farina, Luigi Villoresi, Alberto Ascari and a young former motor-mower mechanic from England named Mike Hawthorn.

Hawthorn had started competitive driving just two years before. He was only 24. Ascari, for example, was 35, Farina 47 and Fangio 42. Hawthorn had flair, he had "touch", he had courage, but he was a novice. Ascari claimed pole-position. Hawthorn was at the middle of the third row.

Gonzalez surged from the start-line at the head of the field, but that had been his strategy. He needed to set up a considerable lead because he had deliberately started with half-full tanks and would have to refuel. Behind him, Ascari, Hawthorn and Villoresi slipstreamed one another down the long straights. First one of them would lead, then another, but, despite their tight teamwork, Fangio prised his way in amongst them. Gonzalez had to refuel on the 29th lap, and now Fangio made his move. On the 30th lap, Fangio led from Hawthorn and Ascari. Less than a second separated the three cars.

Fangio led, Hawthorn led, Fangio, Hawthorn . . . Gradually, the two men drew ahead of the field, but neither could shake the other. Hawthorn recalled later that they were grinning at each other as they roared side by side down the straights. Both men were crouched low to lessen wind-resistance. Hawthorn said that he was so close to the flying Argentinian that he could clearly read his rev counter. Fangio tried every trick that he had learned in his many years of racing to rid himself of this young English whipper-snapper in a bow tie, but Hawthorn clung on like a burr, and as they entered on the last lap, Hawthorn was ahead by a split second. He had deduced that Fangio had lost his first gear, which would give him the edge at the tight Thillois hairpin. Out in the country, Fangio used his extra power to regain his lead, but, as they descended to the hairpin, Hawthorn, using his first gear and his sharper brakes, stole through on the cobbles at Fangio's inside as the latter skidded for a bare moment.

Hawthorn streaked past the chequered flag just one second ahead of Fangio. Gonzalez was third, a mere half second further back. They had been racing at close quarters for 309.4 miles and 161 minutes.

Five years later, Hawthorn would take the World Championship. The following year, he was to die in a car crash.

The World Cup, 1966

It was a golden age in more ways than one. Three of sport's all-time greats – Arkle, Georgie Best and Cassius Clay – were at their zenith. London was swinging. The Beatles appeared to own the Number 1 spot in the hit-parade. Everything seemed possible.

It was only apt, then, that England should host – and win – the World Cup in 1966. They did so in style and amidst controversy. Their names, to those who watched and cheered, will never be forgotten. The Charlton brothers, Bobby Moore, gaptoothed Nobby Stiles, goalkeeper Gordon Banks,

There has been many a memorable FA Cup Final, but none, perhaps, so often and so affectionately recalled as the Bolton Wanderers v West Ham Final of 1923. The most remarkable fact is that it is principally remembered for a four-legged participant.

Wembley Stadium was built to hold 127,000. Some 300,000 turned up on that day and, finding themselves shut out, stormed into the ground by force. It was the coolness and presence of mind of Police Constable George Scorey and his mount, Billy, which saved the day. Together, the veteran of the Boer War and World War I and his white horse calmly drove the wall of humans back to the touchline, and prevailed upon them to sit down.

Though the touchlines were invisible and players found themselves lost at times in the crowd, the game was played. Bolton Wanderers won 2–0. But long after the names of the goal-scorers have been forgotten, the image of Billy confronting a riotous and rancorous mob remains.

Ray Wilson, Martin Peters, Alan Ball . . . and, at the very last moment, snatching glory in two games, Geoff Hurst.

Hurst, the West Ham striker (who also played cricket for Essex), had played five times for England but was omitted for the first games in the World Cup finals. In the 2–0 win over France, however, the great Jimmy Greaves was injured and Hurst was summoned to take his place in the quarter-final against Argentina.

The Argentinians played with a cynicism which, for all their undoubted skills, has unfortunately become their best known characteristic. The German referee was abused at length, but stood firm, booking Argentinian after Argentinian. One player, Rattin, became so incensed that he subjected the ref to a stream of foul-mouthed abuse and, when sent off, refused for eight minutes to leave the pitch.

In the 77th minute, Ray Wilson passed the ball up the left wing to Martin Peters, who fired a cross to the near post. Hurst nodded the ball into the net. England were in the semi-finals.

England would face West Germany with an unaltered team.

Over 400 million people watched that tense, contentious, unforgettable game.

After 13 minutes, first blood went to Germany with a goal from Heller. Six minutes later, Bobby Moore, awarded a free kick, floated the ball towards Hurst, who headed it home.

A great deal of football was played that day. Both the Germans and the English worked tirelessly to break the dead-lock. It was the English who, 13 minutes from the end, succeeded. Ball kicked a swerving corner, Hurst fired a shot which bounced high off a defender. The ball landed in front of Martin Peters, who blasted it into the back of the net.

2–1, then. English viewers and players scented victory. The Germans had no intention of yielding without a fight. They stormed into the England half and, one minute before the end of normal time, they received their reward. Flustered and thrown on the defensive, Jack Charlton fouled Seeler just inches outside the penalty box. The defensive wall formed. The free kick slammed into it. The ball squirted out across the goalmouth, and Weber, finding a gap between Ray Wilson and Gordon Banks, drove it into the net.

We were back where we started. After so much effort, after having been seconds from victory. England could have been forgiven for being dispirited, but Alf Ramsey, the manager, had instilled in his players a unique work ethic. He liked to see them running at every moment of the game and, extra time or no extra time, they would run on till the whistle blew or they dropped.

"You've won it once," he told them, "Now go out and win it again."

Stiles was the manufacturer of that controversial goal ten minutes into extra time. He sent a beautiful long ball up the wing to Alan Ball. Ball crossed to Hurst's feet. Hurst blasted a shot which slammed into the underside of the bar, bounced vertically down and was instantly cleared.

There was a hush where there had been hubbub, as the referee consulted with the linesman. Both deemed that the ball had landed behind the line. The goal was given. England led 3–2.

There seems little doubt that the officials were right, though the evidence on film remains inconclusive. The most telling evidence, as Hurst himself says, is the behaviour of Roger Hunt, who was only feet from the ball as it landed. Had he been in any doubt, he would have followed it in and made sure of the goal. As it was, he turned away, arms uplifted in a gesture of triumph.

Nonetheless, a contentious result would have taken some of the lustre off a great victory. The game, however, was not over. The Germans staged yet another storming counter-attack. In the very last minute of extra time, Held headed the ball across the England goalmouth. Seeler lunged. Had he made contact, the score might once more have been level. As it was, Moore, unflappable as ever, breasted down the ball and moved up the field, beating challenger after challenger. He passed to his West Ham colleague, Hurst, who was just ten yards inside the German half. Hurst, too, neatly breasted down the ball and turned. The German defenders were too tired to challenge him seriously, but Hurst too was almost spent.

The referee was looking at his watch. Three elated supporters were already on the pitch. TV's Kenneth Wolstenholme can be heard on the video soundtrack: "Some people are on the pitch. They think it's all over . . ."

Tilkowski, the German goalkeeper, moved out of the goal. Hurst raised his left foot. The ball streaked into the top of the net.

"It is now!" yelled Wolstenholme above the roar of the crowd.

Freeze-frame, then, on a scene of unbridled emotion:

Stiles and Cohen are crying, hugging, and falling, exhausted, onto the turf. Bobby Charlton is on his knees, as though poleaxed by grief. Alan Ball is doing cartwheels. The crowd is roaring for the engineer of this triumph – "Ramsey! Ramsey!" – and Ramsey is there, hugging his players. Not a cheek that is not smeared with mud and tears.

The Englishman who has forgotten that scene has amnesia.

• chapter two •

SCANDALS

H Company of 2nd Derbyshire Regiment were at one end of the rope, E Company at the other, in the longest tug of war ever. At Jubbulpore, India, on August 27, 1889, they pulled and grunted and grunted and pulled for a total of two hours, 41 minutes before H Company claimed victory.

"The Hand of God"

The Argentinians have long memories. Twenty years after the turbulent quarter-final, they still remembered their disgrace that day and, extraordinarily, held England to blame. The defeat in the Falklands in 1982 also rankled. The world's dirtiest national team was not inclined to give any quarter when England met them in the 1986 World Cup quarter-finals. This time, it was the Latins who came off best. England, spearheaded by an on-form Gary Lineker, had beaten Poland and Paraguay. They were now closer to the coveted trophy than they had been since 1966.

The Argentinians boasted the most gifted player in the world at the time, a playboy named Diego Maradona. For all his undoubted brilliance, Argentina had not mourned when he had left for Europe. His arrogant posturing, his roistering lifestyle and his unpleasant associates had earned him few friends. Arriving in Barcelona to a hero's welcome, his form rapidly declined. His habit of booking entire restaurants and excluding the public did not endear him to the Spanish. When Terry Venables took over the manager's seat at Barcelona, he did the unthinkable. He sold the world's greatest player. No one in Barcelona complained.

And here he was, intent on avenging, as the Argentinians saw it, England's offences.

Five minutes into the second half, Peter Shilton, the England goalkeeper, and Maradona rose as one towards a high cross. Maradona pushed the ball down into the net with his hand. The spectators in the stadium and those watching on television soon knew that it was a handball. Only the Tunisian referee thought otherwise. The goal – an out-and-out, blatant and cynical bit of cheating – was allowed. The sad thing, as was demonstrated magnificently five minutes later, was that Maradona had no need to cheat. He dribbled past man after man and scored with exemplary brilliance. Lineker was to score for England, but the scoreline at the final whistle was 2–1. England were out of the World Cup. With gross cynicism and smugness, Maradona announced that the first goal had been "the hand of God".

An Exhibition

Basketball has long been something of an exhibition sport. The USA have so totally dominated, that it can hardly be regarded as competitive.

From the date of the sport's introduction in 1936, every Olympic final save that in Mexico had been between the USA and the Soviet Union. In 1968, it was between the USA and Yugoslavia. In all of them, America won.

In 1972, however, the Americans contrived to lose. Their previous supremacy makes their petulant, childish behaviour in response still more shameful.

The Russians, to everyone's surprise, ended the first half 26–21 in the lead. As the game wore on, they somehow held on to their lead, though the Americans' constant pressure chipped away at it. With six seconds to go, the USA were just one point behind.

Two Russian errors let the Americans overtake for the first time in the game. Sasha Belov made an inaccurate pass. Collins of America intercepted it. Sakandelize rashly fouled Collins to stop him scoring.

Collins was awarded two free shots. He took the first. He sank it. The scores were even. The crowd stamped and roared. The Russians called a hasty "time-out". Collins shot again. The Americans were ahead for the first time, with the clock showing one second remaining.

Now the Russians protested. Their time-out between the two shots had been ignored. The clocks had gone on ticking. They should have more time.

The Secretary of basketball's ruling body, William Jones, was called upon for a decision. He agreed that the time-out should

Michael Jordan, USA v Lithuania, semi finals, Olympic Games 1992.

have been observed and therefore ordered that the clock should be put back two seconds. His decision, it is generally accepted, was the wrong one. It was the referee's decision nevertheless and, as such, should have been final.

The spirit of amateur sportsmanship, however, had long fled the Olympics.

The Russians had three seconds. Yedesko passed the ball up the court to Belov. Belov caught it, scampered between two defenders and scored.

The Russians had won 51–50. The Americans knew defeat for the first time ever.

Poor little Americans. Denied victory, they stamped and whined and wailed. They protested at William Jones's verdict. A committee convened. It decided in the Russians' favour.

And the Americans – unbelievably, for grown men – were so cross that they refused to accept their silver medals.

Those Pernicious Full Marks

It all started with a little girl named Olga, who stuck out her bottom charmingly and, thanks to tortuous and lethally dangerous training throughout what should have been a childhood, was able to twist her body into some remarkable shapes. This incongruous combination of the sinuosity of a rattlesnake and the dubious charm of Li'l Orphan Annie won for Olga's soi-disant "sport" an enormous following, not entirely composed, we must charitably assume, of paedophiles and sadists.

No matter that, at 17, Olga Korbutt looked to be 11. No matter that she weighed six stones. No matter that she had never been permitted by her "trainers" to acquire the more normal characteristics of a 17-year-old girl. No matter that others, subjected to the same training from kindergarten upward, lay paralysed in clinics back in Mother Russia. No matter that excellence in this sport bore no relation to "fitness", in the sense of fitness to *do* anything, such as fight, run or survive *in extremis*. No matter that we were witnessing child-slavery long, long after we had given it up in the Western world as a bad job. At the Munich Olympics in 1972, Olga captured the hearts of the watching world and had schoolgirls who had hated PE classes mobbing their local gyms.

I hesitate, for all these reasons, to include Olga, or her successor, 14-year-old Nadia Comaneci, in a book devoted to sport. Yet the importance of their performances and the subsequent effect that they had upon sporting standards cannot be denied.

Olga Korbutt came to Munich as a reserve. She stepped in to replace a sick team-mate. She was obviously well-pleased by this, because she emerged smiling and kept right on smiling throughout the Games. On the parallel bars, she excelled. Olgamania had begun. The following day, her performance on the unevens was, to say the least of it, uneven, and the judges awarded her 7.5 out of 10. Olga smiled through her tears.

Now came the individual competitions on each separate bit of apparatus. By now, television had noticed Olga, and her every move was watched by a cooing world.

Well, she messed up the uneven bars yet again, and the crowds got cross when she was, quite properly, marked down. On the balance beam, she shone. She smiled a lot. She stuck out her bum. She inverted herself and contorted herself in smooth lines in a discipline that's only conceivable purpose is mid-wifery for steeplejacks.

As for the floor-exercises – well, there were better gymnasts there, and they executed more difficult contortions and leaps. Olga's performance was conventional – unambitious, even – but there was that bum and that smile, and television commentators the world over used words like "cheeky" and "elan". Olga won her gold. She was the sensation of the Games.

And suddenly circus was deemed sport.

There have long been sports which are judged in more or less arbitrary numerical terms. Ski-jumping springs to mind. At least, however, in ski-jumping, distance is the most important factor. At least the ability to span gaping chasms on skis is related to a genuinely desirable, sometimes necessary, skill. Olga's triumph opened the way for a plethora of seriously silly "sports", arbitrarily judged and entirely useless, of which synchronised swimming is only the worst to date.

Just how silly such sports are was rapidly demonstrated at Montreal in 1976. The gymnastics judges accomplished their own *reductio ad absurdum* in awarding poor little Nadia Comaneci of Rumania seven perfect tens.

What, pray, does it mean, this 10 out of 10, in anything save

an arithmetic test? Surely the terms "perfection" and "human"
are mutually exclusive? And surely the whole history of sport is
the most telling and tangible argument for some sort of
evolution? Year after year, performers excel their predecessors, records are broken, things *improve*. Yet those Montreal
judges, in their overweening arrogance – or, perhaps, realising
the absurdity of endless 9.9s –, deemed Comaneci perfect. They
were wrong.

Eight years later, we had another sensational perfect score,
this time at Sarajevo. Jayne Torvill and Christopher Dean were
the unfortunate victims this time – their sport, ice-dancing.
Quite why ice-dancing should be included in the Olympics
whilst the tango, for example, is not, eludes me, but there it is.
Torvill and Dean put up a brilliant, moving, bravura performance in their interpretation of Ravel's *Bolero*, and richly
deserved the applause, the shower of roses and the subsequent
wealth which that performance earned them. For that matter,
Gene Kelly in countless movies put up brilliant, moving,
bravura performances, but no one gave him Olympic gold
medals, nor perfect sixes; and I suspect that he would have
laughed them to scorn had they done so, pointing out *this*
which he might have improved, *that* which he might have
omitted. *Bolero* earned 12 maximum marks, including a full set
for artistic impression.

Sensation – but for how long? Soon, it is to be assumed, we
will tire of perfect tens or sixes, and will only be satisfied by
scores in excess of full marks. In synchronised smiling, no
doubt.

chapter three

UPSETS

Snooker: The 1985 World Championship

Steve "Interesting" Davis is a thoroughly modern champion. Whereas, in the past, sportsmen have been "characters" with "problems" – drink, women, temperament – snooker star Davis's ironic nickname was earned by a public persona so unexceptional, so mechanically reliable, that he seemed at times to be no more than an automaton. He played in silence and without exhibiting emotion. He destroyed his opponents with what seemed to be ruthlessness. The best efforts of the gutter press could not uncover evidence of the least vice in him. His amusement away from the snooker-table was video games. For a while, he appeared unbeatable.

He had already won the Embassy World Snooker Championship three times, when, as if pre-programmed, he came to the 1985 final at the Crucible in Sheffield.

His opponent, Ulsterman Dennis Taylor, was his antithesis. Davis had a lean and hungry look. Taylor was well-upholstered. Davis was poker-faced. Taylor made self-deprecating jokes as he played. Davis could have been Ken to a Barbie. Taylor looked more like some beaming Toby jug with his huge, upside-down glasses.

Playing with serene precision but without brilliance, great breaks or trick shots, Davis claimed the first seven frames in short order. Taylor smiled ruefully in his corner, apparently resigned to the inevitable.

At the beginning of the second session, it appeared that the match would soon be over. The final is always the best of 35 frames. Davis took the eighth frame 120–0. The watching public sadly anticipated an 18–0 whitewash.

But Taylor won the ninth frame and suddenly looked more confident. He showed real flair in his play. He lost the tenth but squeaked the 11th, 63–48. Suddenly, Taylor was "cogging". He won six successive frames, which included a 100 break in the 15th. At the close of play, Davis led 9–7.

News of the comeback was widely reported, and it was a massive audience that watched television the following afternoon in the hope of seeing Davis beaten. It still seemed improbable, but they dared to hope and pray.

Steve 'Interesting' Davis

Neither man played well in the first session. Taylor won the first frame, then blundered through two losing frames. At 11–8 down, he realised that, until he was seeing the balls better, caution was the best policy. The 20th frame was a model of safety play. Again, it seemed, it restored that much needed confidence. Davis was to have just three scoring shots in the next two frames: 11–11. But Davis's deadpan demeanour reflects strong nerves. He won the next two frames on the black and was leading 13–11 at the end of the session.

It must have been a good night for bars, televisions and TV licence inspectors. 18.5 million people tuned in for the evening session.

Taylor won four frames, Davis two. The scores were level again. Davis then won two frames on the trot, barely allowing Taylor to the table. Three frames remained. Davis merely had to win the next one to claim his fourth world title.

Perhaps the tension affected even Stony Steve. It was a remarkably even frame, but Davis had the chances and failed to take them. A brown juddered in the jaws of the pocket and squirted out again. The last red stopped short. Davis snookered himself off the green. Taylor won 71–47.

He was buoyed up in the penultimate frame and the breaks went his way. He compiled a break of 51 and took the frame 71–24. Again the scores were level, 17–17.

It was going to the wire.

"Softly, softly" seemed to be both men's motto in that final frame. It was to last over an hour. When an obvious chance presented itself, both men took it, then retreated back into safety. Davis potted a lucky green, missed the brown and left the table leading Taylor by 18. There were just 22 points left on the table. If Taylor erred now, there would be no coming back.

None of those shots was easy, particularly in the circumstances, but Taylor went for them and they paid off. Brown, blue and pink went down.

It was all on the black.

Taylor tried to double it into the opposite middle pocket. It was, perhaps, a rash shot, but it nearly came off. The ball bounced back from the jaws.

Each player caught his breath with a safety shot. Davis was aiming to play safe a second time, but hit the ball too hard. The balls skedaddled from cushion to cushion. There was a "click" as the white kissed the black once more. The balls came to rest in line with the pocket.

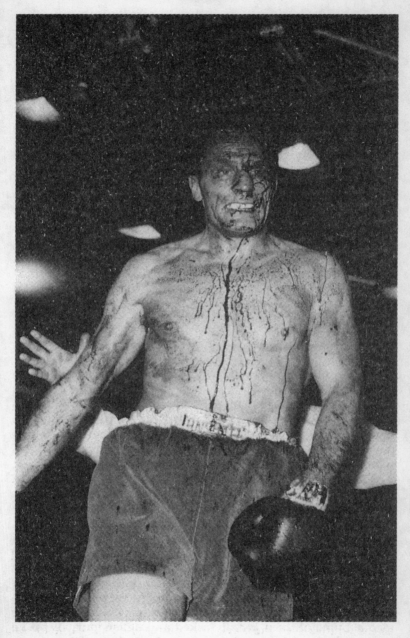

Henry Cooper, during the Henry Cooper v. Cassius Clay fight, 1966.

Taylor had the World Championship in his grasp.

He played.

And missed.

Taylor could not bear it. He did not even see where the balls ended up. You did not make errors like that and get a second chance. Not, at any rate, with Steve Davis around.

In fact, Davis had problems. True, it was a shot which any of the top players would have pulled off nine times out of ten in an exhibition match, but this was no exhibition. The cue ball was nestled near the side cushion. Davis had to execute a tricky cut.

The black had a mind of its own. It was enjoying itself. It did not want to go down. Not yet.

Taylor had his reprieve. Again the balls were lined up with the pocket.

This time, Taylor made no mistake.

A One-Off

It was, we thought, a one-off, a sensation which could never be repeated.

The great England squad, joint favourites for the 1950 World Cup, included such legendary names as Mortenson, Finney, Ramsey, Bentley, Wright, Milburn and Matthews. They and their full-time coach, Walter Winterbottom, travelled to Rio with tails and hopes high. So confident was the FA, indeed, that it ordered Stanley Matthews and Jim Taylor up to Canada, with instructions to fly to Brazil just in time for the World Cup.

The first match was against Chile, a team with only one professional in its ranks. England, without Matthews or Taylor, struggled but managed to win 2–0.

The next game, against the USA, was a formality. The States' team had already lost 3–1 to Spain. Again, Matthews was left on the sidelines. The Americans had no illusions. They knew that they had no chance. Many of them were dancing and drinking until two o'clock in the morning on the eve of the match. Some of them jovially asked an English journalist if he had a cribbage board with him in order to keep the score.

The English team stayed as guests of a British mining company. They changed into their red strips at a hotel near the pitch. They started the game bullishly. They fired at goal. They hit the post. They shot over the bar. They merely had to get their sights aligned . . .

But they met McIlvenny, the Scottish-born wing-half whose greatest distinction to date was seven games for Wrexham. They met unheard of half-backs Bahr and Colombo. Above all, they met Borghi, a former baseball-player, who performed prodigiously in goal. The American forwards were getting little of the ball, but the American defence was fierce. England had their chances, hundreds of them, but they could not finish.

After thirty-seven minutes, the incredible happened. A throw-in from McIlvenny found Bahr who shot at goal from twenty-six yards. Williams, the English goalkeeper, had the shot covered, but Gaetjens, the Haitian, dashed forward at that instant and headed the ball into the net. "Headed" may be a charitable description. There are those who have said that he was dashing in when the ball hit him and that he knew little about it. No matter. The USA had scored against England. The score was 1–0.

And so it remained. The English forwards, merely anxious at first, became frenzied. They drove again and again into the American penalty box, and again and again were repulsed. When the final whistle blew, there were many who sat staring at the rough and ready pitch where the world had just been turned upside down. When the result was telegraphed to the London newspapers, they responded as one with a demand for repetition, clarification – anything sooner than accept the scoreline which confronted them.

The USA never took to soccer, despite this success. A few days later, they were trounced, 5–2, by Chile, and the British returned home with heads bowed.

Those with long memories felt a frisson in 1993, when Graham Taylor's England team travelled to America and the score came across the wires – England 0 USA 1. A nightmare, long thought buried, had returned after forty-three years.

The All Blacks

November 27, 1993.

The All Blacks were back in town. A youngish team. Perhaps not the best ever, we were told by their management. But then, what cardsharp ever boasts about the quality of his poker?

They sure looked formidable enough in their preliminary games, through which they breezed with contemptuous ease. Then came the first of the internationals, against Scotland, and we saw that great rucking and running machine which is the All Blacks. The jocks might as well have been standing before a steam-train waving a Kleenex for all the effect that they had on the New Zealanders.

The scoreline – a gargantuan 51–15 – does not tell it all. It does not reveal the extent to which the Scots, finding themselves powerless, at last just gave up and stood watching, their team spirit shattered. It was the sort of defeat which can break an individual sportsman for years, sometimes for good. You don't recover easily, not when you've just learned that someone else can play the game to which you have given your life so much better that all aspiration is futile.

The Scots I knew took consolation in the knowledge that it was England's turn next week. "The boot'll be on the other foot," they jeered. One even offered me evens against a defeat by 50 or more points.

The auguries were not good. It was England's first match of the season, whilst the All Blacks had been prepared to something like perfection by a triumphant series against the Lions and matches against Australia, Western Samoa and, of course, Scotland.

Six of the England team had two caps or less, Jeremy Guscott was sidelined by injury. The two crucial roles – full-back and scrum-half – were filled by debutants John Callard (at last replacing stalwart Jon Webb, who had retired) and Kyran Bracken.

The famous Maori "haka" war dance looked particularly ferocious that bright Saturday, and few envied the fifteen Englishmen who stood in line to face it.

But from the moment that veteran Rob Andrew kicked off, England were moving forward. Ben Clarke, Tim Rodber, Nigel Redman and Victor Ubogu stormed into the All Black half and their opponents reeled backward. The formerly insuperable New Zealand pair of Jamie Joseph and Arran Pene tasted their own medicine and found it bitter.

Joseph's reaction nearly saw the end of a great dream in the fourth minute. He followed through so late that we, who could suspect no wrongdoing, could only shudder at the state of Kiwi optometry. His foot slammed down upon young Kyran Bracken's ankle. The slight Bristolian, formerly of Skerries, looked as though his game was over. He was heavily bandaged. He hobbled. But he played on – and how he played. He passed long and he passed straight. He was dancing behind the rucks and mauls, slapping and urging his forwards on. He was everywhere.

England's superiority in the line-out was quickly apparent. The All Blacks were held in the scrum, but we waited for the burst of rucks and runs which can sweep the length of a field in seconds.

It never came.

Oh, they tried to run it, all right, but no sooner did the Kiwi gain possession than he was nailed, and nailed the old-fashioned way, hard and low. There were moments when it seemed that we were present at a novel form of tennis-match. Wilson would kick upfield; Andrew would return it; Wilson would kick back; Andrew would return it. It was the only way in which the All Blacks could gain territory, and possession inevitably returned to England in the line-out.

"A spoiling game" the carpers have jeered of England's tactics in the past, as though the spectacle of the All Blacks in full flow were somehow more important and desirable than victory. Well, this was a spoiling game, all right, but it was more. Rob Andrew and his backs were magnificent in defence, but the whole England team set out not just to stop the All Blacks, but to win. They never ceased to drive forward whenever the opportunity arose. To their credit, the astonished All Black backs also stood firm under the onslaught.

Jonathan Callard struck his first penalty after sixteen minutes and another after twenty-eight, whilst the New Zealand kicker, 20-year-old Jeff Wilson, hero of the Scottish game, found today that the posts had narrowed to a pair of stilts. He just could not find the target.

It was to be a scoreline made up of penalties, but the penalties did not make the match. No one who watched could begrudge England their victory. The idea that the New Zealanders were unlucky because their spot-kicker was off-form can only be the product of ignorance, short-sightedness or both. Had New Zealand won because their kicker was on brilliant form, there would have been injustice indeed.

England had three notable chances to score a try. A pass from England's most-capped captain, Will Carling, failed to find its mark but was snapped up by Victor Ubogu and the great Rory Underwood. The ball found its way down the line to Ben Clarke, another of the day's heroes. Clarke made up ground, held on long enough to draw his man, and fed Tony Underwood on the wing. Underwood sprinted for the corner flag. Alas, he had the ball tucked under his left arm. He could not palm off the blistering sideways challenge from the New Zealand full-back, Timu, which might have bought him the extra stride to the line. He put the hip in, but that was never going to be enough for Timu, who felled him as an elephant fells a sapling. A few minutes later, England's smoothly rolling maul approached the line, but somehow Clarke lost possession. Carling was the initiator of the third attempt. He played a lovely long pass to Tony Underwood, who, in what was almost an action replay, again had the ball under the wrong arm and was dragged down by Eroni Clarke.

England's supremacy was so total that, when the first half ended with the score at 6–0, the traditional chorus of *Swing Low, Sweet Chariot* drowned out all other sound.

There was desperation in the All Black's play now. We must remember what the prospect of defeat meant. England had not beaten them since 1983, and had won, indeed, only four times since 1905. Wilson struck a penalty. Callard took his third just one minute later. Wilson scored another three minutes after that. 9–6. No one was relaxing now. England won a fortunate line-out and Andrew dropped a typically cool goal. 12–6

We all knew that the All Blacks had just once to get the machine in motion and a converted try would undo all that hard work. The machine was currently turning over, coughing in readiness to roar. Twice, Tugimala looked to be the one to engage gear. Twice he was checked.

It was Timu – that giant, animated Easter Island statue – who gave us reason to believe that all was lost. A moment's carelessness left the opening, and Timu charged through it. Rory Underwood and Callard were brushed off. He jinked past Ubogu's challenge – it is a mark of the nature of the game that

Ubogu was there to challenge at all – and dived over the line at the corner to touch down.

There was a moment's confusion, then the try was disallowed. Touch-judge Stephen Hilditch had seen that, as he swerved from Ubogu's tackle, Timu's right foot had slid into touch. Timu was sceptical, so were some spectators, but the film evidence unequivocally shows that Hilditch got it right. We could breathe again.

But not too deep. Wilson came back with a penalty to make it 12–9, then the titanic De Glanville, scorning tackles, made a break. The support was good. Andrew continued the run and tried a drop-goal. He missed, but the panicked New Zealanders had run offside. Callard had no problem with the penalty.

Still it was not over. With the All Blacks, it never is. They stormed the England 22 time and again, only to find themselves harried and baulked. At no point did we or the players believe the game won until the final whistle blew.

This was a great moment that will live in our memories because the disadvantaged team played with unique courage and commitment to contain a supposedly irresistible force, and so defied the pundits and the fates.

• chapter four •

MISHAPS AND DISASTERS

Devon Loch

The Grand National was a unique race until the great fences were recently modified. It was unique in that it demanded a very particular kind of horse to win it. Speed and jumping-skill were not enough. A good National horse needed courage, experience, stamina, the ability to mix it in a crowd, intelligence and the will to win. He also needed a large quota of luck. Red Rum won the National an incredible four times, yet his career elsewhere was undistinguished. Mr What won the National in 1958, and thereafter won nothing else. The National demanded a supreme survivor: part racehorse, part eventer, part hunter. It was different.

Now, as the records show, class horses – the sort of horses, in short, who should win the Cheltenham Gold Cup – win the National year after year. Where once it was an open race, now punters can accurately predict the result.

Devon Loch was the class horse in the 1956 National. A grandson of the great Hyperion, he was a fine jumper with a magnificent turn of foot. He was also owned by Queen Elizabeth, the Queen Mother. He was the sort of horse of whom one might say: "If he gets a clear run, he will win." In those days, however, that "if" was a major consideration.

He got his clear run however, Dick Francis had a dream ride. He was sixth as they passed the stands on the first circuit. He was second as they took the Canal Turn on the second. Three out, he took the lead. There was no doubt in any of the watchers' minds that here was the winner.

The run-in at Aintree is cruelly long. None of us who were there will forget – or entirely forgive – the way in which Red Rum ate up the distance between himself and Crisp, the gallant Canadian challenger, who ran a perfect race only to lose in the last strides. Devon Loch's debacle was different. Fifty yards out, he splayed, he foundered, he fell. He lay like a dog, hind and forelegs extended on the turf, while Dick Francis sat bemused and desolate. ESB, ridden by Dave Dick, galloped up, galloped by . . .

There have been many attempts to explain what happened to Devon Loch that afternoon. Some maintain that he attempted to jump a shadow. Dick Francis discounted this theory. He believes that the astonishing roar from the crowd at the

Red Rum jumps the last fence to win the Grand National 1977.

prospect of a royal victory unnerved the exhausted horse. Others believe that the animal suffered a minor heart attack or convulsion.

No one will ever know. Devon Loch had won the Grand National, only to lose it in the last strides.

Le Mans, 1955

We have already seen Mike Hawthorn and Juan Manuel Fangio battling for supremacy in the French Grand Prix of 1953. Two years later, they were at it again, this time in the Le Mans twenty-four hour race. But this time it was to end in tragedy.

The race had started, as usual, at precisely four o'clock in the afternoon, with the drivers sprinting for their cars. Soon the tail-finned Jaguar, driven by Hawthorn, and the silver Mercedes of Fangio were fighting for the lead. Hawthorn was partnered by Ivor Bueb, Fangio by Stirling Moss. For two hours, the battle raged. Then, on the 42nd lap, disaster struck.

Hawthorn led. With Fangio on his tail, he lapped Lance Macklin in the Austin Healey, then pulled across to the right for a pit stop. Macklin had to dodge to the left to pass the slowing Jag. He moved into the path of Pierre Levegh's Mercedes. Levegh, travelling at about 125 mph with Fangio at his rear opted to try to squeeze past Macklin on his near side. There was not enough room. Levegh's Mercedes simply shot up the Austin Healey's sloping tail and smashed into the top of the bank. The front end of the car, with the engine, sheared off and flew into the crowd.

Fangio saw all this, but a moment later, he was past the scene. He did not see the car explode, nor the shards of blazing wreckage which went into the crowd, severing limbs, decapitating, burning and tearing flesh. The ground for sixty yards round was soaked in blood. Eighty people died. Over a hundred were seriously injured.

The race continued, not out of disrespect, but because the organisers reckoned that to stop the race would cause the rest of the quarter of a million spectators to block the roads as they tried to leave.

Alain Prost leads team mate Damon Hill, Spanish Grand Prix 1993.

It was a macabre scene. Darkness fell, and volunteers continued with their ministrations whilst, around them, engines wailed and headlight beams waved like lances.

At two o'clock in the morning, Mercedes received instructions from Germany that they were to pull out of the race as a mark of respect, but still the race continued, and was won by Hawthorn and Bueb.

It was a hollow victory, and the consequences for motor-racing were dire. Mercedes withdrew from motor-racing for thirty-three years. The sport was banned in Spain, Mexico and Switzerland.

Sensational Nationals

Of all the many Grand Nationals, which can be said to have been the most memorable, moving or dramatic? Year after year, there is a new tale of romance, daring, sportsmanship or victory against the odds.

1968's contest was certainly the closest to pandemonium in recent years, and threw up the least likely of winners.

The field was approaching the 23rd fence, the one after Beecher's (and the second smallest obstacle in the race), when a loose horse named Popham Down, who had been flanking them at their near side, suddenly decided to live up to his name. He veered to his right.

Had he practised for years, he could not have timed it better. Baulked horses screeched to a stop and found themselves eating birch. Others, strides broken at the crucial moment, barely rose to the fence and ploughed into it, but without the velocity to push through. Others careered into the melee, to collide with milling loose horses or to be knocked over.

There are sometimes advantages to be had by "laying out one's ground". You get to avoid trouble, for one. It was for no such tactical reason, however, that Foinavon was just skewing over Beecher's as the rest of the field crashed. It had more to do with the fact that Foinavon was very, very slow. He wove his way through the battlefield, took the fence, and jockey Johnny Buckingham found himself blinking, astonished, at an empty Aintree straight.

Robin Smith (l), Ian Botham (c) and Alan Lamb walk back to the High Court after lunch, for the continuation of the case between England and Pakistan cricket teams over ball tampering, November 1993.

As Foinavon plodded on to victory, fallen jockeys were pursuing their mounts. Several were having difficulty in *identifying* their mounts, and climbed aboard the wrong horses. Josh Gifford contrived to remount the favourite, Honey End, and promptly fell again. He nonetheless came in second, only 15 lengths behind Foinavon. Next year's victor, Red Alligator, at length came in third.

1973's race was memorable and sad. It was memorable because it was Red Rum's first victory. It was sad because Canadian challenger Crisp had run, perhaps, the perfect National, jumping like a stag and leading all the way. But the weights and that cruel, extended Aintree run-in were to break him. Red Rum caught him in the very last strides of the race. All of us there felt that an injustice had been done. In time, of course, we would develop an affection for old Red Rum – after his incredible series of wins (he would also score in 1974 and 1977) – but, at the time, there was little love lost for him in the Aintree stands.

Then, of course, in 1981, it was the turn of Aldaniti and Bob Champion. The plot here – an old horse restored to racing by extensive surgery and careful training, a rider recovering from nigh fatal testicular cancer and the horrors of radiotherapy – belonged in a Hollywood script; and was destined to become one, with John Hurt playing Champion in the movie *Champions*.

Perhaps the most sensational of all the sensational Nationals, however, was the one that never was.

The start of 1993's race was delayed by the antics of "animal rights" demonstrators. The old-fashioned starting-tape was sodden when starter Keith Brown at last mounted his rostrum, called the runners into line and pulled the lever.

The tape rose sluggishly. It was immediately apparent that there had been a false start. Brown waved his recall flag, and flagman Ken Evans ran out onto the track to alert the riders. They turned back.

What followed was a shameful fiasco. Again, the now fretful runners lined up. Although Brown must have seen how poorly the equipment had worked the first time, he elected to use that same equipment again rather than opting for a flag start (frankly, it should be said, it matters precious little what method you use to start horses in a four-and-a-half mile steeplechase, so long as you start them). Several of the horses could be seen to have their noses on or over the tape. Nonetheless, Brown – now known in less respectful quarters as

Pierrepoint Brown, after the last official hangman – pulled the lever. The slack tape snaked upward. The horses, as trained, sprang forward. Richard Dunwoody, on Won't Be Gone Long, found a broken length of tape wrapped around his neck as he set off in what is meant to be the world's greatest steeplechase. Had a following horse trodden on the ends of that tape, steeplechasing would have counted itself short one champion jockey.

Keith Brown waved his recall flag . . . but it did not unfurl. For all that we could see, he might have been summoning his gin and tonic from a waiting assistant. As for Ken Evans, he was later to claim that he had been in position and had waved his flag. But many of the jockeys denied that they had seen him, and certainly the video evidence supports the contention that he was not in place.

Several of the riders, despite all this bungling, soon realised that the runners were not off. Dunwoody and Marcus Army-tage, the brilliant amateur who had won the 1990 race on Mr Frisk, pulled up at the first. Former champion Peter Scudamore barely left the start.

chapter five

COMEBACKS

22–24

It could not happen today, not only because of the tie-break system, but also because modern tennis-players, though mighty blasters of the ball, have neither the character nor the skills of their predecessors. Back in the sixties, tennis was a gentler game in which rallies were the norm rather than the exception and delicacy of touch was more important than mere force.

It is generally futile to ask whether a champion of today could have beaten the champion of yesteryear. In tennis, the answer is an unequivocal "no". The power generated by the modern giants with their high-tech racquets precludes tennis as the players of the past knew it. But if we were to set Rod Laver at his prime, say, against the likes of Courier or Sampras in a game where the speed of service was restricted, however, today's champions would find themselves hard-pressed.

Back then, three men dominated the tennis world: Laver, greatest of all time, Ken Rosewall, his fellow Australian, and the Mexican, Pancho Gonzales.

Gonzales was the oldest of the triumvirate. He had been the world's best player in the fifties and, at 33, had retired. His comeback was one of the few in sporting history which really worked. A glamorous, swarthy man of 6ft 3ins, his style was supremely economical. His serve was clocked at 112 mph – and this was with the old-style wooden racquets. He had a volatile temper, generally turned against himself. "You stoopid tennis player" he would mouth as, plucking a sweat-soaked shirt from his shoulder after an error, he returned to the baseline.

At Wimbledon, 1969, this grizzled grandfather of 41 played his way into the record-books.

Gonzales's opponent was a graceful, up-and-coming 25-year-old Texan named Charlie Pasarell. Many appointments were missed in those two days as millions sat transfixed by a battle in which neither man would yield. The opening set, which Gonzales lost 22–24, lasted as long as any whole match played that year. In the second set, Gonzales became irritated by the dying light and lost 1–6. He protested loudly that he could not play in darkness, and was booed off court. The following morning, Gonzales started the climb back. He won the third set 16–14, the fourth 6–3 and the fifth 11–9. In all, the

> Soccer made an unexpected contribution to the resurgence of democracy in the former USSR. The Russian leader, Mikhail Gorbachev, is said to have followed the English League, with particular interest in the doings of Wigan Athletic. He ordered the end of the jamming of BBC transmissions so that he could keep abreast of results.

two men played 112 games and used 13 sets of balls. It was exhausting merely for those of us who watched it. It is a testament to Gonzales's extraordinary fitness that, although he confessed to having cramp towards the end, he continued to battle against his junior and at length contrived to win.

"Humpty"

It will always be known as "Botham's Test" – even, perhaps, as Botham's series. The Somerset giant, who always kept his finest performances for the Australians, was to be man of the match three times in the 1981 tour. He was to bat like some hero of legend confronting enemy hordes, slashing away with disdain. He was to bowl like a lancer. He was to make some of the finest catches. He was everywhere. It may be an exaggeration to say that England would not have retained the Ashes without Botham. It is certainly no exaggeration to say that England must have lost the Headingley Test without him.

Ian Botham was 24. The previous year, he had reached the Test double of 1,000 runs and 100 wickets faster than any man in history. He had been appointed England captain, but the experiment had not proved a success. He had resigned, and now, for the third Test, Mike Brearley returned to the hot-seat. Would Botham resent his return to the ranks? Would he no longer give of his best? Would he hell.

The game started quietly on a grey Leeds day. Australia, one up in the series, finished the day on 203 for three. The second day was still duller, until, after tea, Botham was brought on. He took five wickets for 35 runs. His final figures were six for 95.

4th Test, Edgbaston, 1981: Ian Botham bowls Terry Alderman for a duck.

Australia declared minutes before the close on 401 for nine.

It looked like a draw in the making. An Australian win was conceivable. The third day made it almost a certainty. The great Denis Lillee and Terry Alderman tore into the English batsmen. Only one man – Botham – struck an aggressive and commanding fifty before being caught behind off a rearing, nigh unplayable ball from Lillee. England were all out for a derisory 174. Before the day was done, following on 227 runs behind, they had already lost Gooch without score. It was a rash supporter who now took the 500 to 1 offered in Ladbrokes' tent against an England victory. Ladbrokes had reckoned without Botham.

By late afternoon on the fourth day, England were sunk in gloom. At 135 for seven, 92 runs behind, it seemed unlikely that they could even avoid an innings defeat. The England players had checked out of their hotels. They had reckoned without Botham.

Graham Dilley walked out to join him. The great all-rounder greeted him with a cheerful, "You don't fancy hanging around on this wicket for a day and a half, do you?"

"No way," Dilley replied.

"Right," said Botham. "Come on. Let's give it some humpty."

They gave the Australian attack such ferocious "humpty" that, eighty minutes later, when Dilley was bowled by Alderman for 56, they had put on 117 runs. Chris Old, another left-handed bowler, joined Botham. By the time that he was bowled for 29, Botham had made his century. Of his 103, he had scored 82 in boundaries with 19 fours and one six. Mike Brearley, on the balcony with the rest of the team to applaud the achievement, made a superfluous signal to both batsmen instructing them to stay out there. Botham made a rather more universal signal back. At the close, Botham was still there, accompanied by big Bob Willis. England were 124 ahead. In the two hours after tea, England had scored 127 runs in 27 overs.

The following morning, Willis was soon out. Botham carried his bat with a score of 149, 88 of them scored in fours. England had a lead of 130.

Now another hero stepped onto the scene. Botham had opener Graeme Wood caught behind, but Australia moved smoothly to 56 for one. They needed just 74 to win. Then big Bob Willis, a bowler who until this moment had been a good, hardworking, but perhaps somewhat workaday Test bowler, changed ends to bowl with the wind. He had Chappel caught behind with a blistering, bucking delivery. He proceeded to tear through the Australian team in a state only comparable to the berserk frenzy of warriors in battle. Bright and Lillee made a bold stand of 35 in four overs, but Willis was unstoppable. Australia's last nine wickets fell for 55 runs, Willis taking eight of them.

England had won by 18 runs. This was only the second time in the history of Test cricket that a team following on had triumphed.

Twelve days later, at Edgbaston, with Australia needing just 142 to win with two days to play and ten wickets still to fall, Botham was to take five wickets for one run in 28 deliveries. In the final Test, at Old Trafford, he took three catches, five wickets and scored 118 in one of the greatest exhibitions of aggressive batting ever seen, including six sixes and thirteen fours.

Kim Hughes, Australia's captain, said at the end of the series that the difference between the two teams was represented by one man and one man only. That man, who had brought England to its feet, was Ian Botham.

Celtic v Inter Milan, 1967

There are moments when a great football derby can petrify a city. I have walked about Liverpool on the day of the Everton v Liverpool match and about Turin when Juventus were playing Roma. Both were ghost-towns.

Oh, there were people in the pubs and cafes, no doubt, and people – unfortunates – in the rows upon rows of homes, but no music emerged from the bars, no squabbles from the houses. The normal business of living, the quotidian slanging-matches, love-making, shopping, street-soccer and gossiping were not done. Not while the match was in progress. Later on, of course, the townspeople would make up for lost time in all these fields. For the moment, every eye was turned towards a television, and if a groan or a yell went up, it reflected no connubial release or domestic contention but was echoed in every front-room about the town. A hero on the screen had blundered. A villain had triumphed.

Then, of course, there is the World Cup. That too can engender something akin to paralysis. In Italy and England, of course, this occurs only when the national team has reached the quarter-finals. In Ireland, where I have watched the last two World Cups, it happens every time that the gallant greens take the field. In 1990, the schools were closed and Government Departments ceased to function. In 1993, when Ireland faced their final *qualifying* test, a rare event took place: a motion was carried unanimously in the Dail – "that this house should not sit pending the soccer match". Ireland went ungoverned for two hours.

Local derbies, however, come and go, and there will always be another World Cup. Perhaps the most memorable events, in club football at least, have come in those tournaments where the local lads venture forth, bags laden with phrase-books and cans of baked beans, to face teams with unpronounceable names "on the continent" – the European Cup and the European Cup-Winners Cup.

It is here that the mettle of the fans is most sorely tested. In May, 1967, when Celtic travelled to Lisbon to meet Inter Milan, the Scots did not let their side down. It was an invasion, no less. Lisbon's statuary heroes acquired posthumous decoration in the form of tartan scarves. Guttural noises which, so it was said, had once been Scottish songs, were bellowed to the rafters of the cafes. The British Embassy was packed – after the game, of course – with bemused and bedraggled jocks who had mislaid their passports and their money. It is estimated that 20,000 of them made the trip to Portugal. I doubt that one of them has regretted it.

Inter Milan had been European Champions in 1964 and 1965. Potentially a great side as well as a successful one, their natural flair had been stifled over the years by manager Helenio Herrera, who had turned caution into a philosophy. Entertainment was at the very bottom of Herrera's list of priorities. In the '65 final, against a Benfica side fielding only nine fit men, he had disgraced the game by insisting that, having snatched a one goal lead, his whole team should fall back on the defensive for the remainder of the match. Herrera's own defenders – and they were growing fewer by the day – argued that Inter had suffered defeat only once in the past two years.

As for Celtic, they were in a mood as offensive as Inter's was defensive. Just a few weeks earlier, Scotland had beaten England 3–2 at Wembley – and if there's one thing guaranteed to get a Scotsman's tail up it's the humiliation of England. As for their manager, the great Jock Stein, he was never a man much given to defensive pussy-footing. "Inter will play it defensively," Stein told Hugh McIlvanney before the match. "That's their way and it's their business. But we feel we have a duty to play the game our way, and our way is to attack . . . I mean it when I say that we don't just want to win this cup. We want to win it playing good football, to make neutrals glad we've done it, glad to remember how we did it."

For a long time, however, it looked as though Inter's run-and-hide tactics would again carry the day. In the seventh minute, they won a penalty, and Mazzola had no problem in scoring from the spot. Inter had their lead and, like the man in the parable with his talents, intended to bury it deep. Celtic knew that, 1–0 down, they were facing the greatest defensive team in the world.

They responded magnificently. Gemmell and Craig, on the right and left wing respectively, were so often up front, leading the interminable charges, outflanking their forwards and leaving even Inter's concentrated defence undermanned. Auld was everywhere in midfield, feeding what so often amounted to a six-man forward line. Johnstone produced so many moments of bewildering brilliance. Chalmers must have run a marathon that day.

An hour into the game, the Scotsmen's legs were visibly giving. But Inter looked like Napoleon's troops with Moscow a long way back and Paris still a long way ahead. One minute Gemmell was spurting up their wing; the next, Johnstone was playing circus-tricks in the goalmouth, occupying the attention of three defenders. The ball would be cleared, and there was Craig, eager to apply the pressure once more.

For once, the gods in charge of such things saw justice done. Craig fired the ball back across the goalmouth and Gemmell was there again, this time streaking through the centre. Gemmell struck the ball home with a ferocity quite unbelievable to those who had seen the signs of fatigue in him just minutes before.

Mesmerised, foundering, Inter clung to their discredited strategy. They had no choice. Celtic, reinvigorated, continued the relentless siege. Five minutes from the end, Gemmell again emerged amongst the Italian defenders on the left. He passed back to Murdoch, who shot. The ball was deflected off Chalmers into the corner of the net.

Next year, Manchester United would become the second

British team to take the trophy in a very different but equally
memorable match. But tonight belonged to the Scots, Britain's
first ever European Champions. For hundreds of thousands of
Scotsmen, in the words of the song, "Glasgae", that night
belonged to them. At least 20,011 reckoned that they owned
Lisbon too.

Jessop's Test, 1902

I have recorded elsewhere the Test in which Ian Botham, with
one notable display of aggressive batting, saved a match
already lost. In 1902, another great West Country batsman
had achieved the same feat.

Gilbert Laird Jessop was born in Cheltenham in 1874.
Wonderfully agile and blessed with an eye which would not
have shamed a falcon, he was the greatest smiter of the ball of
his age. He was able to move down the crease to the fastest
bowlers and pull or drive them. He also ranked high in the fast
bowlers lists and was perhaps the finest fielder of his time.

The auguries for the fifth Test at the Oval were not propi-
tious. England had already lost the series. After a mid-order
and tail-enders' bonanza, Australia scored 324. Heavy rain fell
on the morning of the second day. England struggled on a
sticky Oval wicket to score 183, again after spirited stands by
lower order batsmen.

Trumper threw away his wicket at the outset of the Australians' second innings. Lockwood bowled well, and dismissed the tourists for the second time for a total of 121.

On Wednesday morning, then, England set out needing 263
to win. The pitch was breaking up now. Saunders and Trumble,
for Australia, made good use of it. The first three wickets fell to
Saunders for ten runs. Half the side had been skittled out when
Jessop – "The Croucher", as he was known – joined Jackson in
the middle. The outcome at this point looked to be a foregone
conclusion.

At first, Jessop appeared to be in poor form. He struggled,
and offered two missed chances. At lunchtime, Jackson was on
39 and Jessop, 29. After lunch, however, the two men seemed to

swap roles. Jackson became bogged down whilst Jessop started
to wield the bat in a manner which was not to be witnessed
again in Test cricket for another 81 years. At one point, he hit
four fours and a single off successive balls from Saunders. The
partnership had added 109 in just sixty-five minutes when
Jackson was caught and bowled by Trumble. It was not too
long before Jessop fell to a catch with the score at 187. He had
scored 104 of the 139 runs made during his stay at the crease.

The spectators could hardly bear to watch. 49 to win, and
three wickets to fall.

Hirst, the senior remaining batsman, was inspired by his
predecessor and batted bravely whilst Lockwood and Lilley
came and went. At 248 for eight, with only 15 needed to win,
Lilley drove a catch to deep mid-off.

Everything depended on Hirst and the last man in, Wilfred
Rhodes. Wilfred Rhodes was then known as the world's
trickiest slow bowler. In time, by sheer application, he would
be a partner, with Jack Hobbs, in one of the great opening
partnerships. For the moment, his number eleven position
reflected his batting ability. Today, however, he rose to the
occasion and imperturbably scored in clever singles. Once he
gave a chance to Armstrong at slip and England held her
breath, but Armstrong dropped the catch.

Rhodes scored the winning run and Hirst carried his bat for
58.

Nine years later, in a county match, there was to be another
display of aggressive batting which defied belief, not least
because of the unexpectedness of the man responsible.

Edward Alletson, number nine for Nottinghamshire and at
best a workaday bowler, went in against Sussex with his team
in trouble. With seven wickets down in their second innings,
Nottinghamshire were only nine runs ahead. Some god possessed Alletson that day. Before lunch, he took fifty minutes to
make 47. Afterwards, he made 142 out of 152 for the last wicket
in just forty minutes! His last 89 runs were scored in fifteen
minutes! He hit the ball out of the ground twice. He scored six
other sixes, and 23 fours. Sussex had to make 237 in three and a
quarter hours. They failed to do so.

Alletson never scored another century, nor excelled in any
game.

Nigel Mansell

Why do Jews play the violin? I once wrote to Yehudi Menuhin to ask him, and he couldn't offer an answer. Yet the fact is that every great fiddler in history – Paganini, Kreisler, Zuckerman, Stern, Oistrakh, Menuhin himself – has been Jewish – until the last few years, when, still less probably, the Japanese and the Koreans have moved into the market.

There are some things which Britons do well, too, and no one can really tell us why. Why should Britons excel at the two-man bob, for example, when snow in Britain rarely falls more than enough to ruin other sports? Why should Britain, in which ice occurs only on roads and in water-pipes, boast a pantheon of skaters and ice-dancers such as Curry, Cousins, and Torvill and Dean? Why should we consistently produce milers, such as Bannister and Coe, yet rarely produce distance-runners and, still more rarely, sprinters? Why marksmen, when many nations have a greater tradition of shooting?

And why, perhaps above all, should Britain over the years have been the principal single cradle of great motor-racing drivers? Just consider the list: Segrave, Moss, Surtees, Hawthorn, Hailwood, Clark, Hill, Stewart, Hunt and Mansell are just the first of many that come to mind.

It may be that we will never know just how great a Formula 1 champion Nigel Mansell might have been. He has now been lured away to Indy car racing in the States by bigger bucks and, perhaps, by a little less politicking. Already, in his first year, he is World Champion in his new sport. Perhaps that tells us just how good he might have been.

Two moments in Mansell's career stand out in the mind above all others. One, in Adelaide back in 1986, was a crushing moment of defeat. The other, at Silverstone in 1992, was a moment of nigh riotous jubilation.

Mansell came to the Australian Grand Prix in 1986 needing to finish third to clinch his first World Championship. If his Williams team-mate, Nelson Piquet, or McLaren's Alain Prost won this race, and Mansell finished out of the frame, his dream would be dashed. It seemed unlikely.

It seemed still less likely when Mansell claimed pole position over Piquet, Senna and Prost. Mansell, however, made a poor start, and was soon in fourth position behind his former team-mate, Keke Rosberg, and the two men whom he could not allow to win.

Piquet went into a spin. Mansell drew up to take his place. He only had to retain that third position to have the title in the bag. Prost dashed into the pits to replace a punctured tyre. All four tyres were replaced. The technicians calculated that, had it not been for that puncture, Prost could have completed the race on the one set.

That was enough for Williams. They decided to allow Mansell to race on without a tyre-change.

Rosberg had to retire because of tyre damage. Piquet now led. Prost, who had been making up ground after his tyre-change, had overtaken Mansell to seize second place. Mansell was third.

Rosberg's misfortune had alerted the boffins. Williams's two drivers must, after all, have a tyre change.

They realised it, but they realised too late.

Mansell put his foot down on the Brabham Straight – and disaster struck.

He was travelling at well over 150mph when that tyre exploded, shooting off flaps of rubber and showers of sparks.

A car travelling at that sort of speed without a rear tyre is less predictable and more convulsive than any living creature. Mansell had to control a car jerking and veering like a demented bucking bronco. Every jerk could have turned into a careering spurt into oblivion, but somehow Mansell kept control. He would never have taken his wounded car around the right-angled bend ahead, but he saw an escape road and somehow coaxed the car in. He hit the concrete wall. The front wheel was shorn off, but the car ground at last to a halt.

Mansell has, at times, been criticised for a lack of charisma. He is of that new breed of professional sportsmen who give total dedication and apparently emotionless single-mindedness to their game. Emotions were shown that day. There were tears on his face as he walked away from his wreck of a car.

Emotions were shown six years later, too. In the British Grand Prix, Mansell was driving what had by now become unquestionably the fastest car in the world. Again he got off to a bad start, letting his team-mate Ricardo Patrese outstrip him. By the end of the first lap, however, Mansell was three seconds ahead of Patrese. He had only to hold on to that lead to score his seventh win of the season (incidentally beating Jackie Stewart's record of 27 Formula 1 wins) and to make the World Championship his bar the shouting.

Mansell did not drive like a man with a clear lead. He drove like a man challenged at every bend and with something to prove on every straight. By lap 20, he had extended his lead to twenty-two seconds. On the penultimate lap, he broke the lap record again. He was racing against a phantom car and a phantom driver. He was racing against himself.

The British fans who stormed the track at considerable risk to life and limb had further cause to celebrate. Martin Brundle in the Benetton came in third after a classic mid-race scrap with Brazilian Ayrton Senna.

The World Championship was Mansell's bar the shouting, I said, and so it was; but, amidst the thousands of Union flags that fluttered about Mansell's car that day, there was a lot of happy shouting yet to come.

The Greatest Collapse – the Greatest Recovery!

We hear only too often of England collapses in cricket, when, it seems, the rattle of wickets is heard almost as often as the smack of leather on willow. The following scorecard, however, tells of a collapse and a comeback unequalled in first-class cricket. Warwickshire batted first for a respectable total. Hampshire were then all out for just 15. A foregone conclusion? Not in cricket. Following on, Hampshire proceeded to knock up a staggering 521 to win by 178 runs. The century-scoring tail ender, Livsey, by the way, earned his living as Lord Tennyson's valet.

WARWICKSHIRE v HAMPSHIRE

Birmingham, June 14, 15, 16, 1922

First innings:
WARWICKSHIRE

L.A. Bates c Shirley b Newman	3
E.J. Smith c Mead b Newman	24
Mr F.R. Santall c McIntyre b Boyes	84

W.G. Quaife b Newman	1
Hon F.S.G. Calthorpe c Boyes b Kennedy	70
Rev E.F. Waddy c Mead b Boyes	0
Mr B.W. Quaife b Boyes	
J.Fox b Kennedy	4
J.Smart b Newman	14
H.Howell not out	1
Extras	2
	203

HAMPSHIRE

A.Bowell b Howell	0
A.Kennedy c Smith b Calthorpe	0
Mr H.L.V.Day b Calthorpe	0
C.P.Mead not out	6
Hon L.H.Tennyson c Calthorpe b Howell	4
G.Brown b Howell	0
J.Newman c C.Smart b Howell	0
Mr W.R.Shirley c J.Smart b Calthorpe	1
Mr A.S.McIntyre lbw b Calthorpe	0
W.H.Livsey b Howell	0
G.S.Boyes lbw b Howell	0
Extras	4
	15

This staggering scorecard tells so many stories. Were it a chess game, it would be spiky with exclamation and question marks. Starting with the accidental poetry of "A.Bowell b Howell", it records an afternoon of unparalleled gloom. How often can a batsman going in second wicket down have carried his bat with just 6 runs? What a cheer must have gone up as Mr Shirley scored his one run! We can imagine the Warwickshire players' jubilance as Howell and Calthorpe led them back to the pavilion with figures of six wickets for seven and four for four respectively, having skittled out a top-class side in just 8.5 overs. If they were incredulous then, the match's marvels were not yet done.

Second innings:
HAMPSHIRE (following on)

A.Bowell c Howell b W.G.Quaife	45
A.Kennedy b Calthorpe	7

Mr H.L.V.Day b Calthorpe	15
C.P.Mead b Howell	24
Hon L.H.Tennyson c C.Smart b Calthorpe	45
G.Brown b C.Smart	172
J.Newman c&b W.G.Quaife	12
Mr W.R.Shirley lbw b Fox	30
Mr A.S.McIntyre lbw b Howell	5
W.H.Livsey not out	110
G.S.Boyes b Howell	29
Extras	27
	521

On this occasion, Howell returned figures of three wickets for 156, Calthorpe, two for 97 and Quaife, three for 154! Hampshire can have entertained little hope of victory at 186 for six, but Shirley and Brown made a stand of 85 and Livsey chose today to make his first century. Brown, in all, batted for nearly five hours.

WARWICKSHIRE	
L.A.Bates c Mead b Kennedy	1
E.J.Smith c Shirley b Kennedy	41
Mr F.R.Santall b Newman	0
W.G.Quaife not out	40
Hon F.S.G.Calthorpe b Newman	30
Rev E.F.Waddy b Newman	0
Mr B.W.Quaife c&b Kennedy	7
J.Fox b Kennedy	0
J.Smart c&b Boyes	15
H.Howell c Kennedy b Newman	11
Extras	10
	155

It is sad that Alfred, Lord Tennyson was no longer around. The achievements of his grandson, his son's valet and George Brown must surely have warranted an heroic ode.

chapter six

STAYING POWER

Liverpool in Europe

It is 30 May, 1984. The all-conquering Liverpool team has come to Rome. They have already taken the League Championship and the Milk Cup. Now they seek to crown this *annus mirabilis* with victory in the European Cup Final.

But Liverpool are tired, and tonight they face Roma, before a fiercely partisan crowd. Oh, there are Liverpool fans here, but they are hugely outnumbered. In Liverpool, football may be the second religion. In Italy, it tops the list. The walls of the Vatican, so close at hand, must tremble at the roaring from this Olympic Stadium.

Every Italian schoolboy knows the Liverpool team almost as well as his own champions. He has watched the progress of Souness, Rush and Dalglish with a discerning and critical eye through the hard-won triumphs at home and through the four previous matches, all of them away, all of them tough, which Liverpool have won by sheer grit and grinding hard work. Their football has sometimes been unlovely, but they have proved themselves the greatest team in Britain. Now they stake their claim to be the greatest in Europe.

The schoolboy, however, will see tonight as a blank sheet on which history will write itself. For us, whatever may befall, it is a paragraph at the foot of a gloriously illuminated page.

Eight years ago, in this stadium, on this turf, we saw another Liverpool team trotting out beneath the floodlights. We can see them still if we close our eyes. This was Bob Paisley's Liverpool – Keegan, Clemence, Kennedy, Hughes, Neal – and they too had come to a European Cup Final after a long season. They too were a team of fighters rather than dancers.

But whereas tonight's Liverpool arrive already festooned with victors' laurels, that Liverpool came here direct from defeat in the Cup Final. Whereas tonight's transplanted Kop is dwarfed by the local fans, the Liverpool supporters that night, 26,000 of them, exuberantly claimed this stadium for their own.

Their opponents were Munchen Gladbach.

Was it the simple fact of being away from home which freed that Liverpool to play such devastating, devil-may-care, attacking football? Or was it just that, having lost at Wembley, this was an all-or-nothing event for them? For, from the first

Bjorn Borg on his knees in thanks as he wins the Men's Singles for the third consecutive time, centre court in the final of the Wimbledon Championship 1978.

whistle, this sometimes pedestrian, if always effective, team did not scamper and scurry; it swept smoothly forward in probing attacks, feinting, parrying, falling back to regroup, seeking the weak spot in the Gladbach defence whilst always containing their attacks. It was a Liverpool revitalised, a Liverpool reborn.

27 minutes into the first half, the reward came. We can see them still on the floodlit turf. Callaghan to Heighway; Callaghan, Kennedy and Case spurting forward in feinting runs to draw their men; Heighway running on, slipping the ball to the momentarily unmarked McDermott, who put it, almost casually, into the net . . .

Then, half an hour further in, disaster as Case blundered; Simonsen, who had been waiting for half such a chance for the past hour, did not need asking twice.

For a while, then, Gladbach looked dangerous, and the great Ray Clemence had his work cut out. But Hughes was urging on his men and Keegan, in his last match for Liverpool, was running a marathon in short spurts, harrying and worrying and opening up space. The Liverpool dominance was reasserted. A floating corner from Heighway, and Tommy Smith, also in his last match for the club, found a way through the massed green of Gladbach to head it in. Then the coup de grace, a Phil Neal penalty.

The red-scarved fans, armed only with beer-cans and goodwill, stormed through the streets and piazzas of the Eternal City like Visigoths turned hippy . . .

And what was it Emlyn Hughes said then? "What the hell do we do for an encore? The treble? No way . . . we are the team of the century . . . and no side will ever get nearer. It can't be done . . ."

Those boys down there are trying to prove him wrong, and they are making a fair job of it. Roma are having to work to keep the red strips out. After only a quarter of an hour, Johnston centres perfectly, and it is somehow only right that it should be veteran full-back Phil Neal who pounces upon the rebound off Tancredi and slams the ball home.

Tancredi is hard-pressed now. Souness scores, but the goal is disallowed. Rush and Nicol both blast at goal, but the 'keeper thwarts them . . .

But the tide is turning. Increasingly, it is the local team which is moving forward; Liverpool must mark and contain as best they can whilst falling backward. Now Tancredi can take a well-earned breather. It is Grobbelaar who must earn his keep.

He earns it, all right, with fine, gallant saves, but it cannot last. The equaliser comes when Conti finds a barely visible gap between Neal and Lee. He lofts the ball across the goalmouth, and Pruzzo rises to head it in.

The second half. A milling game, in which neither side seems to believe that it has the ability or the right to win. There are moves in both directions, but weariness seems to have deprived the strikers of their killer instinct. There is a lot of work being done down there, a lot of hard running and tight marking, but again and again the ball is cleared from one goalmouth or the other. The whole game has taken on the air of a rather frantic dream.

Extra time. The dream continues, only now it has elements of nightmare. Both teams are exhausted. They play on, it seems, out of conditioned reflex. Still there are chances which set the crowd upon a roar, but again and again the chances are wasted or missed.

It is the final whistle which awakes us all. Suddenly, there is a high-voltage buzz where before there were raucous and ragged cheers and jeers. Suddenly, down there, all is bustle.

Now history will be made in more ways than one. For the first time ever, this tournament will be decided by a penalty shoot-out.

It is not a satisfactory method. It is not even particularly fair. But it's all there is, and perhaps it's to Liverpool's benefit. One wonders if even they could have endured a replay – yet another harrowing final of this importance, this intensity.

To our astonishment, it is Steve Nicol, called on as a substitute for Johnston, who first steps up to the spot to have it out with Tancredi. He shoots. The ball skews high above the crossbar. Tancredi merely watches it go.

Di Bartolomei faces Grobbelaar. He scores.

Neal steps forward. Eight years earlier, against Gladbach, it was he who put the matter beyond doubt with a penalty. He has already scored Liverpool's one goal in this game. He could so easily undo all the good that he has done. But his nerve holds. The net billows.

Righetti confidently hits back for Roma, Souness for Liverpool.

2–2, then, but Nicol's misfire may still cost Liverpool dear. Dalglish and Johnston are off the field. They still have Rush to come, but the Italians have their two World Cup stars, Conti and Graziani, in hand.

Conti goes next. He fails.

It is rare that a groan can drown out a cheer, but the groans of Roma's supporters make the mini-Kop inaudible. It is as though they'd taken the Hollywood Bowl for music-hall night and Conti had just told the one about smoking after intercourse. Level-pegging, then, but Liverpool still have it all to do. For Rush, it is a formality – or, at least, he makes it look like one. Graziani's turn. Grobbelaar reads him right.

A miracle is in the making.

It is left to Kennedy, the only other remaining veteran of that team which trounced the Germans, to settle Roma's hash for once and for all. Tancredi goes the wrong way.

Liverpool have completed the most formidable and taxing campaign in football history. They have fought battle after battle. Now, at the last, shell-shocked and battle-scarred, they have won their greatest victory in single combat, champion v champion.

"It can't be done" Emlyn Hughes had asserted. No one, surely, can ever have been happier to be proved wrong.

Desert Orchid

Desert Orchid was not a great horse.

I'm sorry, and I know that it will shock the many hundreds of thousands who came to love him, but the truth must be faced. Desert Orchid was a very, very good horse. He was touched by that indefinable quality which marks a star. He was as full of guts as any horse that I have seen since Mandarin, who won the French Grand National with a broken bit, finding his own way over the fences, his own way home.

To be honest, I have never quite understood why it so shocks the fans to be told that Dessy was no Arkle, no Golden Miller. Is it so shocking to learn that John Wayne, say, or Cary Grant, was no Olivier? Desert Orchid, too, captured the imagination of the public and had a style all his own. Above all, he was one hell of a fighter.

He left us in no doubt of this last quality when, on hock-deep ground in the Cheltenham Gold Cup of 1989, he at least refused to admit that he was not a great horse.

The race organisers had considered abandoning the day's sport because of heavy rain the night before and snowstorms that very morning. They left it until midday to decide that, mudbath though it might prove, the Gold Cup would be run.

Richard Burridge, Dessy's principal owner, had, perhaps, a harder decision. His "people's champion" – to borrow a phrase from snooker-player Alex Higgins – carried the good wishes and the sentimental bets of a million friends and fans. Dead ground was one thing. The slippery morass which Prestbury Park had become was quite another.

Burridge, however, was an intelligent owner – the sort that trainers quite properly pray for. He left the decision to his trainer, David Elsworth. Elsworth decided, not without misgivings, to go.

The mud made it a test of stamina and courage from the outset. Carvill's Hill, the Irish invader, put down at the seventh and crashed. Golden Freeze, Slalom and The Thinker, the Gold Cup winner of two years earlier, were also casualties that first time round. Desert Orchid, under his habitual rider, Simon Sherwood, made the pace throughout that first circuit, but Sherwood let his mount take a breather. Ten Plus took it up.

Three from home, Ten Plus met his fence all wrong and came down. Alas, he broke a hind fetlock in the fall and had to be destroyed.

The crowd did not know that, not then. All that we knew was that the beloved grey was in the lead again. The dream was intact. Few of us, however, believed that it would remain so. The conditions were too taxing, the uphill run-in too merciless, and here came Yahoo, upsides for a few strides, then overtaking.

Over the last two, Yahoo retained his lead, but Dessy hung on desperately, never once setting back his ears, never once conceding. He was leaning in the straight like a supermarket trolley, but Sherwood shook him up, straightened him, urged him on.

To give up would have been the work of a split second – a faltering step, a short stride, a momentary glance anywhere but straight ahead. It never entered Desert Orchid's head. He held on. He wore the presumptuous challenger down, and, in those final strides which should have been his undoing, he pulled ahead.

And here, I believe, he showed much in common with Arkle, with whom he has so often and so wrongly been compared for other reasons.

Dessy had had it easy in his time, if never as easy as Arkle;
but, when he had to fight, he pushed himself to the limit. And,
fanciful as it may seem, anyone who ever saw Arkle run knew
that they were watching a performer. He pricked his ears at the
roar of the crowd. He basked in adulation. He put in giant leaps
just because he was in front of the stands. I said that Desert
Orchid was a star, and this is part of it: the star's love affair with
his fans. I'd swear that the cheering of those people gave Dessy
that extra few inches.

Ten Seconds

Defeat is always cruel but nowhere, perhaps, more than in the
100 metres. All that effort, all those years of training, all the
assiduous dieting, all the psychological build-up, all the sacri-
fices can be thrown away in less than ten seconds. You slip on
the blocks. You can't find your rhythm. You don't peak at the
right place at the right moment. And your name, which might
forever be cast in gold, is cast instead into the mists which await
also-rans.

Linford Christie suffered that fate at the Tokyo World
Championships in 1991, and he felt that he couldn't go on. It
would be so much easier to go back to the old way of life –
rum-soaked all-night parties with friends, the occasional club
sprint just for the fun of it.

For that had been Christie's life until he was well into his
twenties, when he developed the conviction that cutting down
on the rum and increasing the running might actually pay
dividends. He had been right, in a way. He was the fastest
sprinter in Europe now. But who needed the strain, the pain,
the uncertainty, just for this?

Fastest sprinter in Europe, after all, meant little when there
was always a faster American on the big day. And, tonight,
there had been three faster Americans – Carl Lewis, the
bugbear of Christie's career, who had just won in a world
record 9.86 seconds, Leroy Burrell and Dennis Mitchell. Christie was 31, four years older than any Olympic sprint champion
in history. Where was the point in continuing?

And not only that: tonight he saw with terrifying clarity the fate of also-rans. In coming fourth, he had established a European record of 9.92 seconds. Yet no one was celebrating; no one was congratulating him. It was win or nothing. And how was he to win?

Well, the mood passed. Christie's coach, Ron Roddan, pounded some positive attitudes into Christie's head. Revenge would be sweet at the Barcelona Olympics . . .

But every dog has his day, and August 1, 1992, was to be Christie's. Lewis, thanks to the rigorous American selection regulations, was not a contender. He had finished only sixth in the Olympic trials and was in town only as long-jumper and relay runner. Burrell had hit a bad patch in his career. Mitchell, too, was not at his best. Maybe Christie's dreams were not, after all, so fantastic.

The starting-line and a loaded gun. Only one of these human bullets will hit the tape and bring home the bacon. The rest will be spent bullets, no more.

After all the preparation, it is small wonder that there were two false starts. Christie seemed to stay cool. Again the gun rapped, and they were away. Or not. Christie cannot have known for certain that this was it, the moment, but he must break and run as though the hounds of hell were at his heels.

For a moment the Canadian shows in the lead, then the runners in the middle have made an arrowhead of the field. Christie's blue lycra-clad thighs are up there amongst them, ahead of them. Arms pump. Teeth are bared. Eyes are screwed up tight.

The tape flies.

And it is done.

Christie knows. The Jamaican-born immigrant's first impulse is to grab a Union flag from a spectator and to set off on a jubilant lap of honour.

As for the defeated, they are prostrate.

That is the difference between winners and losers in the Olympic 100 metres.

chapter seven

RECORDS

Jesse Owens

Jesse Owens will always be remembered as the athlete who wiped Hitler's eye at the Berlin Olympics. The stadium was draped with swastikas. The Fuhrer was present in person to witness the supremacy of the Aryan race and the Germans in particular. The Nazi press sneered at America's "black aux-iliaries".

They did not sneer for long. Within one week, Owens won the 100 metres in 10.3 seconds. He was then pitted against one of Hitler's champions, Luz Long, in the long-jump. It was a hard-fought battle, but Owens took the gold medal with a final leap of 8.06 metres. The 200 metres followed. Owens beat his countryman Mack Robinson by a staggering four metres. In the 4×100 metres relay, Owens set up a five metre lead for his team-mates on the first leg. They went on to win in a world record 39.8 seconds.

On May 25th, just over two months earlier, however, Owens had produced a still more remarkable set of performances. He was competing for Ohio State University at Ann Arbor, Michigan. At first, he was reluctant to run and jump that day. He had injured his back in a wrestling romp with another student and was afraid that he would not do himself justice if, indeed, he could get off the starting-line at all. His coach persuaded him. Owens took a hot bath and resolved, no matter what, that he would relax this afternoon.

At 2.45, the gun went off for the start of the 100 yards. 9.4 seconds later, he broke the tape. He had equalled the world record.

Ten minutes later, Owens lined up for the long-jump. There were nineteen other competitors, and Owens had undertaken to run in the 220 yards a quarter of an hour later; he resolved that he had time for just one jump. He had a scrap of paper placed 26 ft. 3 ins. – the world record – from the take off board. He then jumped.

The 21-year-old student picked himself up 26 ft. 8¼ ins. from the take off. That record would endure for 25 years.

There was little time for celebrations. Owens won the 220 yards in 20.3 seconds, then the 220 yard hurdles in 22.6 seconds. In the space of one hour and fifteen minutes, Owens had equalled one world record and broken five.

Owens was to turn professional at 22, but his contributions to amateur and Olympic athletics were not over. At a track and field event in Philadelphia one day, a little boy of ten was brought over to meet the legendary, now middle-aged athlete. A photograph was taken of Owens with the boy. Owens signed it.

The boy was "Carl" Lewis, who was to emulate his hero in an almost identical feat forty-eight years later in Los Angeles.

Jack Hobbs

There are sportsmen who appear and disappear with all the speed and all the dramatic effect of a great comet streaking across the night sky. There are others, rarer by far, who truly merit the appellation "Stars" in that they seem to possess not merely the brightness but also the apparent permanence of heavenly bodies. Stanley Matthews was one. He played his first full season for Stoke City in 1932. He was not to take home an FA Cup winner's medal until 1953, when he played a dazzling and essential role in Blackpool's 4–3 win over Bolton Wanderers (Blackpool had been 3–2 down until three minutes from time!). By then, he was 38 years old and the most famous footballer of all time. The newspapers must have had their retirement tributes, if not their obituaries, ready for some years. They were to moulder in the archives for another twelve

> The biggest fish ever caught on rod and line was probably a 2,350 lb shark, caught by Bob Dyer in Moreton Bay, Brisbane, in June, 1958. Other record monsters include an 852 lb tunny (J.H. Lewis, Scarborough, 1949), a swordfish of 1,040 lbs (Zane Grey, Tahiti, 1930) and a blue mako of 998 lbs (F.H. Low, New Jersey, 1935). The biggest brown trout ever caught was the great Loch Awe fish of 39½ lbs (W.C. Muir, 1866). The record salmon in British waters weighed 64 lbs and was caught in the Tay by Miss R.M. Ballantyne in 1922, whilst the biggest Norwegian salmon weighed in at 74 lbs. It was caught in the Tana by Lensmann in 1879.

astonishing years until Matthews finally called it a day, still at
the top of his game, in 1965.

Modern sport, of course, allows no such longevity. From the
moment the swimmer takes his first dive or the tennis-player,
newly out of Pampers, strikes his first ball, he is aware that his
days are numbered. No less than those striped-shirted, sus-
pender-wearing, yapping lads who traded commodities and
inanities in the eighties, the sportsman is a professional under
constant pressure. Obscurity is certain. All that counts is
whether it should be rich or poor obscurity.

Jack Hobbs never seemed to be under pressure. He was a
professional in an age of amateurs, but he firmly believed that a
cricket eleven should be captained only by a gentleman and
never aspired to grandeur or to luxury in his own life. It must
be an enduring cause for sorrow and incredulity that this great
batsman, whose eye remained sharp and his smile bright from
1905 until 1934, was nonetheless a lifelong teetotaller. Despite
this, he played at the highest level and with extraordinary
consistency from the last days of Fry and Ranji to the heyday of
Bradman.

Which are the Hobbs moments which best qualify for
inclusion here? The brilliant 178 (including twenty-two
fours) which, in a partnership of 323 with Wilfred Rhodes,
nigh destroyed the Australians at Melbourne in 1912? The
100th century in first-class cricket scored at Bath in 1923?
Certainly that was a memorable day, and, like Matthews's
Cup Final, drew plaudits with a decidedly valedictory tone.

In those days of longer and fewer matches, this was, by any
standards, a fantastic achievement. Only W.G. Grace – with 126
– and Tom Hayward – 104 – had previously attained it. It came,
too, at a moment when Hobb's side, Surrey, most needed it.
They had batted badly in the first innings, leaving Somerset
with a lead of 49. Returning to the wicket, Surrey looked likely
to repeat their disastrous performance. They lost Sandham,
Ducat and Shepherd – the last two to Somerset's sharp throw-
ing – for a total of 36, and the score had reached only 45 when
Mr Fender was leg-before. Four wickets down, and four runs
yet to score to equal Somerset's total.

Hitch came in, and suddenly Surrey were scoring. Hobbs
reached his 50 in two hours, and the partnership went on to
make 121 in just over an hour and a half before Hitch was
caught behind. With complete control, never offering so much
as a ghost of a chance, Hobbs reached his century in a total of

three hours five minutes, having scored the final 50 in sixty-five minutes. Surrey declared at 216 for five.

And that, it was assumed, was that. With "we'll never see his like again" on their lips, clubmen prepared for Hobbs's inevitable benefit and honourable retirement.

Hobbs did not see it that way.

In July, 1925, we find him with a dozen centuries already under his belt for the season and his total standing at 125 – just one below Grace's record. And there, as so often happens, he stuck. He made high scores, but could not move into three figures. Until, once again, he faced Somerset, this time at Taunton.

A huge crowd gathered to see the great man move into the higher reaches of legend. Hobbs took guard, played a couple of balls, and was caught at cover-point. Or so it seemed to the spectators who had not heard the umpire's cry of "No Ball!" Again, on seven, Hobbs played a careless – or nervous – shot down the leg side, and was lucky to escape dismissal. This case of "the yips", as golfers call such uncharacteristic behaviour, was short-lived. From now on, Hobbs showed typical caution where appropriate and flamboyance where allowed. He was in command. He finished the day on 91.

He was not going to allow nerves to get the better of him the following day. He attained the century in the first over, and for many minutes there was no further play. Every player on the pitch had to shake his hand, and his captain brought out a bumper with which to toast the crowd.

Of course, it is another commonplace that the man who has attained the long-sought triumph too often loses his concentration and is at once out. Such was Hobbs's fate. He was caught for 101.

He was not, however, prepared to allow his series of centuries to suffer the same fate. Less than thirty hours after equalling Grace's record, he surpassed it in the second innings. He scored another 101, this time unbeaten, in a 183 first wicket partnership with Sandham which lasted just two hours and thirty-five minutes. By scoring his fourteenth century of the season, Hobbs also broke C.B. Fry's record of thirteen in a season.

Again, the pundits polished their superlatives and dug a deep hole for their hero, then had to jump into it themselves. The following August, against Middlesex at Lord's, Hobbs hit 316 – the highest score hit at HQ to this day – in six hours and fifty-five minutes of apparently faultless batting. Meanwhile, Hobbs and Sutcliffe scored 2,300 runs between them in the matches against the Australians. One of these matches was the memorable final Test at the Oval, where Hobbs scored 100 and Sutcliffe 161 in the second innings, bringing the Ashes home for the first time in 14 years.

In 1930, the 22-year-old Don Bradman first came to England, and, in an unforgettable display of virtuoso batting in the Third Test at Headingley, hit a century before lunchtime on the first day, and went on to score 334. In the process he notched up his second consecutive double century in Test Matches, his third consecutive century, his first 1,000 runs in Test cricket and his 2,000 aggregate for the season. At last, one feels, Hobbs, opening for England with his famous partner Herbert Sutcliffe, must have seen the writing on the wall. That writing was forcibly underlined when, in England's second innings, Hobbs set off for an easy run to hear the clatter of his wicket. The arm which had so brilliantly hurled the ball? Don's, of course.

Hobbs played on for a further four years. Remember those farewell tributes when he hit his hundredth hundred? By the end, he had scored 197 centuries and a total of 61,237 runs.

Roger Bannister's Four Minute Mile

In all track and field events, there is a magical mark – of no significance in itself, but sought by practitioners like a grail. Of these, none possessed more mythic desirability than the four minute mile.

Successive athletes had whittled the mile record down to 4 minutes, 1.5 seconds, the time scored by Gunder Haeg of Sweden in 1945. And there, for nine years, the record had stuck, on the very threshold. The more it defied aspirants, the more it became, as it were, taboo.

Three young men with no such respect for bogies decided to have a tilt at the record on May 6th, 1954. They were Chris Brasher, Chris Chataway and Roger Bannister.

Bannister was 25 and a medical student at Queen Mary's,

Paddington. He had been training for this day since he had run the mile in 4 minutes 2 seconds a year earlier.

The attempt was carefully planned. It was to take place at Oxford University's Iffley Road ground. Brasher would set the pace. Chataway, a 5,000 metres specialist, would take it up. Bannister would supply the barnstorming finish.

It worked like clockwork. It was a gusty day, and for a while it was thought that the attempt might be abandoned, but the wind was measured and was within the permitted limits. The attack was on.

Brasher could have been an automaton, the way he set the perfect pace – 57.4 seconds for the first 440, 1 minute, 58 seconds for the 880. Bannister urged him to go faster. Brasher paid no attention. He was right.

Chataway took up the lead for the third lap and for most of the fourth. There were less than 250 yards to go when Bannister kicked as though the hounds of hell were at his heels.

"I drove on, impelled by a combination of fear and pride," he later wrote. "My body had long since exhausted all its energy but it went on running just the same . . . Those last few seconds seemed never ending. The faint line of the finishing-tape stood ahead as a haven of peace after the struggle. I leaped like a man taking his last spring to save himself from the chasm that threatens to engulf him . . ."

"The time is three . . ." announced the commentator, and no more was heard above the bellowing of the crowd.

In fact, Bannister's time was 3 minutes, 59.4 seconds.

The barrier was broken. Within two months, Australian John Landy ran the mile in 3 minutes, 58 seconds. Bannister was to beat Landy later in the season in 3 minutes, 57.8 seconds.

Laker, Lock and Shackleton – The Year of the Bowlers

One year, from August 1955 to the end of July 1956, was to witness four of the most extraordinary bowling feats in cricket history.

On August 17th and 18th, 1955, Derek Shackleton of Hamp-

Mark Spitz races through the Olympic pool to break the 200 metres
butterfly record, 1972

shire skittled out Somerset for 37 in the first innings and 98 in the second. In the first, his figures were eight wickets for four runs in 11.1 overs, surely among the very best ever recorded. In the second, he returned a comparatively wasteful six for 25.

This achievement was eclipsed – to some degree unjustly – by two startling sets of figures attained by Jim Laker, the Surrey and England off-spinner, against the Australian tourists. For his county, he bowled for four and a quarter hours, getting all ten wickets for 88 runs in 46 overs, 18 of them maidens. In the second innings, Tony Lock, Surrey's other spinner, finished with an analysis of seven for 49. Surrey became the first county team to beat the Australians for forty-four years.

Twenty days later, against Kent, Lock was to take all ten wickets in an innings for just 54 runs in 29.1 overs, and, all told, returned figures of 16 wickets for 83.

Not to be outdone, at the end of that July, Laker took nineteen Australian Test wickets – the only time that anyone had ever achieved this feat in a Test match, and the most wickets ever taken by one man in a first-class match.

This was an astonishing match for many reasons, not least of which was the fact that the first five England batsmen – Richardson, Cowdrey, Rev. David Sheppard (now Archbishop of Liverpool), May and Bailey – were all amateurs. This had not happened since 1899.

England won the toss and elected to bat. Richardson and Cowdrey gave magnificent displays of strokeplay and made 174 for the first wicket. Both batsmen were out within half an hour of each other, and Peter May and David Sheppard continued to score smoothly. The pitch was unresponsive to speed or to spin, though, towards the close, it appeared already to be breaking up. Richie Benaud was able to get one leg-break to lift and dismissed May, but, at the close, England were 307 for three.

The next day, England continued apace. Sheppard completed a flawless century, and wicket-keeper Godfrey Evans laid about him with a will for 47. In all, England made 459 runs in 491 minutes.

Australia began their reply just after half-past two. Before stumps were drawn on the second day, they had lost eleven wickets. After an opening stand of 48, Laker and Lock pinned them down. Lock was to break the opening partnership immediately after tea. Thereafter, Laker began his destructive work. The last eight wickets fell in thirty-five minutes for 22 runs. Laker's spell after tea brought seven wickets for eight runs in 22 balls.

Australians like to refer to the English as "whinging Poms", but they can whinge with the best when things don't go their way. That night, they complained that the pitch had been prepared expressly for England's spinners. It was a fatuous complaint, and by Tuesday evening all such words were being eaten, together with a deal of humble pie. Because the grounds-men at Old Trafford could not be held to blame for what happened next. It rained. Only three-quarters of an hour's cricket was possible. Sunday and Monday were wet and windy. In all, one hour's cricket was played on the Monday, during which Australia moved on to 84 without further loss.

The nightmare was that, after achieving so much, England might be robbed of their well deserved victory by the clock and the weather. The following day, however, the rain had checked and the wind had dropped. Play started just ten minutes late. The pitch was slow and damp. McDonald and Craig dug in for the draw. At lunch, the score was 112 for two. They had to hold out for just four hours more.

After lunch, the sun peeked through. The ball began to spin. Laker took four Australian wickets for three runs in nine overs, three of them without addition to the score. Benaud joined McDonald then, and they made a stand until tea.

England had to get four wickets in an hour and fifty-five minutes. McDonald, after a sterling innings, was caught off the second delivery after the interval. The seventh, eighth and ninth wickets fell. Still victory was not certain. It was 5:27 when at last Maddocks was given out lbw. England, thanks largely to Laker, had won by an innings and 170 runs.

Bob Beamon's Flight

It was a freak, an extraordinary jump with no precursors. It happened at the Mexico Olympics in 1968 and it happened to an American jumper named Bob Beamon. I say "it happened" because it is impossible to believe that Beamon "did it" in the sense that he planned or aimed at the mark which he achieved.

Somehow, all the muscles combined to make this exceptional jump possible.

Lynn Davies, Britain's 1964 gold medallist, was in that long-jump final. So were joint world record holders Igor Ter-Ovanesyan of the Soviet Union and Ralph Boston of the United States. The world record stood at 8.35 metres.

Bob Beamon had had a good season. He had beaten Boston on several occasions and had scored 8.33 metres. Today, however, did not look to be his day. He jumped two no-jumps, then played safe. He took off some 30 centimetres in front of the board and registered an unimpressive 8.19 metres. Boston, meanwhile, broke the Olympic record with a leap of 8.27.

There was a shower of rain. The athletes broke for lunch. The final resumed with three foul jumps. It was Beamon's turn.

And it happened.

Beamon floated. He soared. He flew from the ground as if from a springboard. He came to earth *beyond the scope of the measuring device*. A tape had to be introduced. Drop-jawed athletes watched, shaking their heads as if doubting their eyes. They doubted their ears next, as the distance was at last announced.

Beamon had jumped 8.90 metres: 29 feet 2½ inches. That was 55 centimetres further than any man had ever jumped before.

Even Beamon could not believe it. He was gabbling and crying: "Tell me I'm not dreaming. Tell me I'm not dreaming . . ." That record looked set to stand for half a century, but the pace of progress in athletics has never been faster. It stood through the seventies and eighties but finally fell to Mike Powell, who, in the Tokyo World Championships, cleared 8.95 metres.

Mark Spitz's Seven Golds

Being brought up in Hawaii, it was only natural that Mark Spitz should swim. It was *how* he swam – the ease, the fluent rhythm – which, from the earliest, drew the eye. When the family moved to Sacramento, California, several observers pointed out that this talent might be something very much out of the ordinary. At nine, therefore, young Mark started training at the Arden swimming club. His father, a scrap merchant, took it in turns with his wife to get up at 5 o'clock in the morning to take their young son training. The rabbi objected. Swimming was taking up time better devoted to Hebrew studies. Mark's father, Arnold, announced, "Even God likes a winner."

The word was spreading. George Haines, the Olympic swimming coach, took one look at the boy and knew that here was a champion in the making. He took him under his wing. This necessitated a move for the family and a change of school for Mark, but already it was plain that it was worth it. While still at High School, Mark broke his first world records. He was a natural, but even naturals have to work. Mark was swimming at least 26 miles a week at racing-pace, and spending over 20 hours a week in the pool. He was fit. He was exceptionally gifted.

He was, frankly, cocky.

He approached the 1968 Mexico Olympics with something like complacency. After all, success had been easy for him throughout his life. In the two previous years, he had set twenty-eight US records and ten world records. He is said to have predicted that he would bring home six golds.

He had a lesson to learn.

In the 100 metres butterfly final, Spitz, the world record holder, was up against his countryman, Doug Russell. The contest was thought to be a foregone conclusion. It had happened so often before. Russell had blistering early pace, Spitz a devastating finish. Overall, Spitz was the faster.

So what perverse impulse caused Spitz, in this, the most important race of his young life to date, to adopt his rival's natural tactics and leave nothing in the tank for the finish? It was Russell this time who, unable to believe his luck, bided his time and took gold.

It got worse and worse. The unfamiliar taste of defeat seemed to cause Spitz to sicken. In the final event, the 200 metres butterfly, Spitz, again the world record holder, finished last. His time was over *eight seconds* slower than his own record. He returned to Sacramento chastened and dispirited, with just two team golds to his name. In addition to his personal chagrin, of course, he had to face the mockery of the press, never slow to cut an over-confident upstart down to size.

Four more gruelling years' work on his swimming and his

temperament, and Spitz again stood on his blocks for an Olympic 200 metres butterfly final, this time in Munich, at a Games which will be forever marred by the kidnap and murder of Israeli athletes by Arab terrorists. Spitz surged through the water, surged up at the end in triumphant salute. He had won gold, and had scored a world record with a time of 2 minutes and 0.7 seconds.

The roller coaster began later that evening, in the 4×100 metres freestyle relay. Spitz swam the last leg – another gold, another world record.

The following day, in the 200 metres freestyle, Spitz scraped home with another world record; two days later, he made a procession of the 100 metres butterfly, beating his nearest contender by half a second – another world record. One hour later, the USA 4×200 metres freestyle relay team lifted another gold in world record time, with Spitz again swimming the last leg.

Now Spitz again showed a lack of character – or, perhaps, of maturity. Justly protective of his unbeaten record at the Games, he was reluctant to face a genuine threat in the form of Jerry Heidenreich in the 100 metres freestyle. This unsportsmanlike, self-absorbed attitude was rightly scorned by Spitz's new trainer, Sherm Cavoor.

Spitz conceded, but was plainly unhappy. He was only the third fastest qualifier for the final. In the race itself, we thought for a moment that we were witnessing a replay of the last Olympiad's debacle. Spitz set off at an untenable pace from the gun.

Heidenreich was not phased. He kept in touch, and suddenly Spitz was foundering. The smooth rhythm which characterised his finest swimming had fled. Now, however, he dug deep within himself and found resources of courage and stamina such as he had never had to call upon before. He touched the wall a fraction of a second before the powerful Heindenreich. It was another world record.

Number seven posed no such troubles. It was a formality. In the medley relay, four swimmers must swim one hundred metres – two lengths – in different strokes. There was a momentary flash of hope for the East Germans as Roland Matthes set a world record for his backstroke leg; the Britons had cause to cheer as David Wilkie swam a blinder in the breast-stroke. Then Spitz hit the water for the butterfly and it was all over bar the shouting.

There was plenty of shouting.

Seven golds, seven world records – no, eight, because, of course, no one had ever won so many Olympic titles at one Games. It is doubtful that anyone ever will again.

chapter eight

THE GREATEST EVER

Arkle: Death and Disaster at Kempton Park

Let's face it. The futile conversations are the most fun, because we can practise them. They are never resolved. We return to them as we return to old friends with whom we can be at ease because we know them so well.

"Would the Miller have beaten Arkle?" is a fine subject for such late night debate.

Arkle – let's start the discussion with a suitably contentious assertion – was the greatest steeplechaser of all time. He would have trounced the Miller. This is not to say that Golden Miller was not a great horse. Compare the winnings: Arkle won £75,206, the Miller just £15,030. The influences of sponsorship and of inflation negate these figures. Arkle won three Cheltenham Gold Cups; the Miller won an incredible five. The Miller won a Grand National; Arkle was never permitted by his adoring owner, Nancy, Duchess of Westminster, to participate. The Miller broke three track records – at Liverpool, Cheltenham and Lingfield. Arkle broke just one, at Sandown.

The figures argue against Arkle, but . . . Well, Arkle trounced Mill House, one of the finest steeplechasers ever seen on a British racecourse, and trounced him not once but many times. Thomond, the Miller's hottest opponent, was good, but not, I think, that good. Consider, further, that the rules of racing had to be changed to accommodate the phenomenal Irish animal.

Arkle could give three stones and a thrashing to Mill House, a horse who must have won three Gold Cups without his rival's presence. He could give two stones to Fort Leney, a Gold Cup winner, and leave him standing. He won three consecutive Gold Cups, three Leopardstown Chases, two Hennessys, a Whitbread and an Irish National.

Only Mill House had previously won all four legs of the "big four" – the Hennessy, the King George VI, the Gold Cup and the Whitbread. Arkle not only repeated the performance, but humiliated Mill House in the process. The five lengths difference between them in the '64 Gold Cup became 28 lengths (and 3 lbs) in the '64 Hennessy, 20 lengths in the '65 Gold Cup and 24 lengths (and 6 lbs) in the Gallaher of 1965.

Not only that, but I, in common with all others who saw

those races, can attest that Arkle won them with many, many lengths to spare. He was looking about him as he raced, showing off. He was a born performer. When he did break the Sandown course record, in the Gallaher of 1965, it was by seventeen seconds, and still he was going away in the final furlong.

If Golden Miller was greater, I do not believe in Golden Miller.

Others have concentrated on Arkle's Gold Cups. I remember rather those two Boxing Days in 1965 and 1966 when Arkle won, then lost, the King George VI Steeplechase at Kempton.

Mill House stayed away from that '65 race. There was no point in his racing against Arkle now. There was a hoar frost. The sky was dark grey, relieved only by streaks of pale light. A dustbin lid seemed to have been slammed down upon us all.

Snaigow and Rondetto, finding that Arkle stayed in, had declined to run. That left Dormant, 15–1 (although he had won last year's Whitbread and Mildmay), Artic Ocean, a novice who had won two 'chases and who started at 100–1, and Dunkirk, a two-mile specialist – in steeplechasing terms, a sprinter. Last March, Dunkirk had won the two-mile Champion Chase at Cheltenham and, in November, the Mackeson. In the same month, he had established a two-mile course record at Ascot in a time *four seconds faster than the hurdle record* and faster than the *average flat time!*

Dunkirk's owner, Colonel Whitbread, was a sportsman. Some would say that he was reckless. He set out to test Arkle

Dorothy Paget was the archetypal eccentric millionairess. She lived in an entirely female household and lived, furthermore, largely by night, sending memo after memo to her many secretaries and drivers at all hours. She had many public rows with the trainers of her huge, and hugely expensive, string of racehorses. Consequently, those horses had many trainers. She drove, or was driven, to the races at phenomenal speeds, and would take over the racecourse restaurant, where she would eat gargantuan quantities.

In her one shapeless hat and her tubular coat she became a familiar and much-loved figure to the British racing public. For all the millions which she ploughed into racing, she was rewarded with little success. The only exception was Golden Miller, the only contender for Arkle's crown as the greatest steeplechaser ever.

by setting his two-miler to establish a phenomenal lead, thus dispiriting the champion and forcing him into blunders.

The race was of three miles.

Arkle started at 7–1 on.

Dunkirk, piloted by Bill Rees, took the race to Arkle. He set off at a ferocious pace and, at the end of the first circuit, had opened up a lead of 20 lengths and more. Pat Taaffe and Arkle were unconcerned. They declined to get flustered. And now, as they swung round into the back straight, the familiar yellow, chocolate hoop colours broke from the pack.

It was literally terrifying to watch Arkle drawing in the rope. He left Artic Ocean and Dormant standing. He made it look as though Dunkirk was moving backward. At the fourteenth fence, the gap was seven lengths. Dunkirk pecked. They were nearing Dunkirk's optimum two-mile mark. Pat Taaffe clicked on. He rose to the fifteenth in front.

Dunkirk was not to rise to that fence. He met it dead.

Is it too fanciful to believe that the horse's heart had burst? He had just run the race of his life. By rights he should have been being patted and feted. Instead, this beautiful monster, Arkle, was cruising ahead of him as though at a hack canter.

Dunkirk ploughed into the birch. His hind legs swung upward like a diver's, upward to the vertical – and on.

For all the darkness of the day, there was no doubt in our minds that Dunkirk was dead. As for Bill Rees, he was flung forward. As he lay on the turf, one thousand, one hundred pounds of horseflesh swung towards him like a headsman's axe. It shattered his right thigh.

Arkle won by a "distance" – a huge distance at that – and seemed bent on doing a further lap of honour. Pat Taaffe had a hard time pulling him up.

The following Boxing Day, there was to be more drama. The massive weights which Arkle was being asked to carry in handicaps – weights greater than any horse had ever been asked to carry – were beginning to tell. He had won the third of his Gold Cups (he was to win them by an aggregate of 45 lengths!) but, in the Hennessy, had failed to give Stalbridge Colonist 2½ stones and was beaten by just half a length. At least here, at Kempton, the most he would have to give away was 21 lbs.

Woodland Venture, a mere six-year-old, was considered Arkle's nearest rival. No consideration was given to Artic Ocean, nor to Scottish Final or Foinavon (a horse who had the knack of being in on great upsets). *The Times*, however, noted that Dormant was "ominously well-treated at the weights" on 11 stones.

Arkle set off in his usual cocksure, casual style. Dormant headed him at the tenth, but Arkle shrugged off the challenge. Behind Dormant, Woodland Venture was going easily; Maigret, an ex-point-to-pointer, was a length behind.

As they reached the fourteenth, we waited for Arkle to move into overdrive and shed his contenders. Arkle skewed over the fence. Woodland Venture was in the lead. Pat Taaffe had to work at Arkle to regain the front. We waited. When would Arkle break away? When would that familiar surge start?

It never came.

Woodland Venture and Terry Biddlecombe crashed at the second last. Arkle led. He jumped the last badly, but nothing, surely, could catch him in the last furlong.

But Arkle was struggling. It was clear now. There was something wrong. Jeff King, on Dormant, was using his unequalled strength to push the animal along. He was gaining.

He caught Arkle a stride from the post. He passed it a full length ahead, so slowly was Arkle travelling. Mrs Wells Kendrew, Dormant's owner and trainer, was gleefully clapping and cheering beside me in the stands. A few minutes later, she was in tears as the news came through that the best loved champion in racing history had pulled up lame. He had broken the pedal bone in his hoof, but had raced on as best he could. To the list of Arkle's virtues we now had to add great courage.

He was never to race again. In May, 1970, at only thirteen, because of painful stiffness in his hind quarters, he was put to sleep.

At the 1969 Horse of the Year show, in his last public appearance, Arkle had trotted into the arena to a tune chosen by his devoted owner. The tune was apt: "There will never be another you".

Two Immortal Tries

At another point in this book we saw how the All Blacks recently met their match at Twickenham for only the fourth time since New Zealand v England tests began back in 1905. No doubt there were old men who, as they watched that great triumph, found their thoughts drawn back to another unexpected England victory on that same turf fifty-seven years before, the first against New Zealand.

You didn't need to be that old to make the connection. Everyone of us that ever played Rugby Union has seen that game, played on 4 January, 1936. One of the coach's means of inspiring the team was to unroll the cinema screen, switch out the lights and set the clanking and whirring projector rolling. And up there, in jerky, speckled black and white, we would watch the match which will always be known as Obolensky's Game. It still had power to astonish, to motivate and to fill us with awe.

It may be supposed – such was the brilliance of Prince Obolensky's two immortal tries – that the two England victories, separated by half a century, were very different. After all, in the 1993 game there were no tries, and England won by sheer bloody-minded, confrontational teamwork. The concentration upon the young Russian's running, however, perhaps belies the true nature of the earlier game. England would have won the Obolensky game without him, just as, had England boasted an Obolensky in 1993, they would have won by a greater margin.

Again, as ever, the All Blacks' game was one of rapid rucks and swift, orderly running and passing. In full flood, it seemed impossible to dam them. The England policy back then was therefore the same as that of Will Carling. Carling was to say that "confrontation" was the key; the England supremos in '36 ordered that the All Black forwards should be "pounded and shaken". The packs were equal in the set, but New Zealand were always faster and more efficient in the loose. Finding themselves closely marked and well pounded and shaken, that advantage was negated. They swept like the cavalry upon the squares at Waterloo and found themselves checked at every turn.

Nor were the English content to play a defensive role. Led by Peter Cranmer of Richmond who again and again stormed through the centre, twice to make tries, once to drop a goal, England went on the offensive.

Cranmer banked the fires, Obolensky supplied the spark.

In the face of relentless pressure, England took possession from the loose, Gadney passed out to Cranmer, and the ball passed swiftly and neatly down the line of running backs.

Obolensky was some ten yards from touch on the right wing and just inside the England half. He sprinted for the corner.

Obolensky was so much more than just a runner. He had the skill to lengthen his stride or to fade at just the right moment to wrongfoot a challenger. He was close to the touchline when Gilbert sped towards him, ready for the tackle. Had Obolensky been hit or had he taken normal evasive action, he would have been tipped into touch. He did neither. At precisely the opportune moment, he found overdrive. Gilbert looked frankly stupid, as he clutched at thin air. But Gilbert was anything but stupid; he was a fine football player. I doubt, on reviewing the evidence, that anyone could have done otherwise. One moment, the man was there; the next, he was past.

So the battle went on, and, as in the recent game, the New Zealanders were loath to give up their unbeaten record. Only moments later, they piled down on the English line, but the white-shirted forwards and backs somehow stood firm against the tide of black and the ball was cleared.

In the 39th minute, history was made.

This is the reason why coaches still roll out that grainy film: to demonstrate not just skill but courage and formidable footballing intelligence. It was Cranmer who set it all up again. He blasted through the New Zealand centre, then passed out to Candler. Candler could pass no further out to the wing because All Blacks Ball and Gilbert stood in his path.

Suddenly, Obolensky appeared at Candler's *inside*, swift as a sliver chipped from the England line. He took the pass from a surely bemused Candler and ran for the opposite corner flag. Again he eluded all challenges with that sweet variation in pace, and touched down in the left-hand corner, having described an impossible, cross-pitch diagonal.

Coaches pass over the attempted conversions. England's place-kicking was abysmal that day. Half-time came, and England led 6–0. The feelings of spectators were no different from those of their successors in '93. We were ahead, but for how much longer could we remain so? New Zealand returned revitalised. They smashed into the English defence, and few believed that the home-team could withstand the onslaught. Yet withstand it they did, and kept on coming back. A scrum . . . a loose ball . . . Cranmer was on it, thought to run, thought better of it, and precisely drop-kicked the ball between the posts.

Still England could not feel safe. Two converted tries, after all, would equalise the scores, and two converted tries at no

point seemed impossible. But England were gaining control
and winning more possession in the line-outs and the scrums.
Once the All Blacks made it back into the England half; again it
was Cranmer who made the most of a loose ball, smashed
through the New Zealand line and passed to Sever who scored
a straightforward try between the posts.

The game was over, but the New Zealanders, as ever, did not
know it until the final whistle blew.

Pedal Prestidigitation

There was just one missing ingredient in the World Cup of 1966
– a genius unparalleled in the history of soccer who, by an
accident of birth and in consequence of the curious rules of
FIFA, which counted the Soviet Union as one nation and Great
Britain as four, qualified only to play for Northern Ireland.

Year after year, the newspapers will herald with fanfares of
superlatives "the new Arkle" or "the new George Best". They
are deluded. There is, there will be, no such thing.

How can anyone who saw Best, trickling like some intrusive
liquid through apparently stationary defenders, compare him
with, say, that lachrymose lump, Paul Gascoigne? Best's
balance was beyond belief, his speed bewildering, his control
over the ball such that you blinked, as at an illusion, trying to
work out how the trick was done. This is no nostalgic reverie.
You can find the proof positive in your video shop today. You
will witness sleight of foot – pedal prestidigitation – which
inspires as much awe today as it did back then.

George Best was discovered and tutored by Matt Busby, the
much-loved, dogged manager of Manchester United. Ten years
previously, "Busby's Babes", the great United team of 1958, had
been almost wiped out by an air crash at Munich. Now Busby,
still with some of the veterans of Munich in his team, was back,
contending with Benfica in the final of the European Cup.

It would be pleasant to relate that so great a game was played
in sporting and Corinthian style. Alas, it was not so. From the
outset, Best was a marked man. The Portuguese carved him up
and hacked him mercilessly but, for all his delicacy of touch, he
was no frail flower. The referee was a disgrace to his noble

Linford Christie, 100 metres Gold, 4th World Athletics Championship, 1993

Gordon (later Sir Gordon) Richards rode the last winner at Nottingham on October 3, 1933. He proceeded to ride all six winners at Chepstow the following day and five more the day after – a total of 12 consecutive winners. He retired in 1954 having ridden 21,834 horses, 4,870 of them winners. He had been champion jockey 26 times. His 269 winners in the 1947 season remains a record, even though, in his day, it was impossible to jet to two meetings a day.

calling, on one notable occasion giving a foul against United's Crerand for viciously attacking Eusebio's knee with his testicles. This was too much for Nobby Stiles, never a respecter of referees, who decided to see if Eusebio could similarly foul him. Only captain Bobby Charlton prevented full-scale battle.

There was no score at half-time. United were frustrated by the Portuguese fouling, Benfica by United's staunch defence. In the second half, United took the game to Benfica. In the 53rd minute, Sadler crossed and Charlton flicked the ball into the net with his head.

One minute later, Best broke loose. That he dribbled the ball past every defender in succession is a matter of fact. *How* he did so remains a mystery. He scored with outrageous ease. The Italian referee called it offside. Manchester fans called the Italian referee all sorts of things. The referee was wrong. The fans were right.

Victory, however, still seemed in prospect when, ten minutes from the final whistle, 19-year-old Brian Kidd bungled. The ball was pounced on by the Portuguese and Graca drove it home.

The game went into extra time.

Stepney kicked the ball up into the Benfica area. The ball was passed to Best. The Beatle-cropped maestro had another sudden infusion of godliness. He jinked. He skipped. He sidestepped. With fantastic insolence, he disdained the shot and instead wrongfooted the goalkeeper, as he had wrong-

On 5 October, 1974, Mike England and John Pratt, playing for Tottenham Hotspur, both scored own-goals in the first half of their match against Burnley. In the second half, both scored for their own team.

> The result of the Astley Stakes at Lewes in 1880 was a dead heat
> between Scobell, Wandering Nun and Masurka, with Cumberland
> and Thora a head back, dead-heating for second place.

footed the other ten players, and tipped the ball into the back
of the net.

From that moment onward, the thudding and roaring did
not let up. Nor did United.

Brian Kidd, having given away the Portuguese goal, was not
having a happy 19th birthday. Until, that is, United ran through
the Benfica defence like cavalry through foot-soldiers, the ball
rose before him, he headed, and the roars of the faithful
redoubled.

Six minutes later, Kidd's nightmare became an impossibly
sweet dream. It was he who supplied the centre to Charlton,
who struck a typical, if sublime goal. At the final whistle, the
triumphant players slumped down onto the Wembley turf after
their 4–1 victory. The thunderous roars of the crowd continued,
the red-and-white scarves swung in the darkness, and Matt
Busby and the Benfica players stood applauding.

Grundy and Bustino

Flat-racing is seldom a sport for poets. It would, perhaps, be
unjust to maintain that it is a matter merely of one horse
running faster than another – a public test of value for the
subsequent bloodstock market – but that, in general, is the long
and the short of it.

It is unfair, of course, but for all the silks and the haute
couture and the vast sums of money entailed in flat-racing, it
rarely has the glamour of the winter sport nor so captures the
imagination of the sporting public. In part, of course, this is
because steeplechases are longer and more interesting than the
average race on the flat – "It takes longer to lose your money, so
you get better value" as one noted punter told me. In part, it is
because the champions on the flat have such woefully short
careers. You can come to love an Arkle, a Mandarin or a Desert
Orchid; but with a flat champion, who retires in his fourth year

Gareth Edwards, Sydney, 1969

to perform more pleasant and private duties, the racegoer's relationship is more in the nature of a one-night stand. And last, of course, there is the matter of the jockeys. Jump-jocks can be big, roistering, hard-drinking heroes. The average flat-rider, existing on a wafer and a cup of tea a day, does not, for all his skill and courage, fit the heroic mould.

Just occasionally, however, there have been fleeting moments on the flat which remain etched on the memory as clearly as a great 'chaser's whole career. Dancing Brave's blistering burst to take the Arc (in a final hundred yards which would have left the finest sprinter standing) still defies my belief, though I have watched it a hundred times. Nijinsky's triple crown and the sheer brilliance of Mill Reef, Sea Bird and Shergar will never be forgotten by those of us privileged to see them.

Great battles are even rarer. One towers above the rest.

Grundy, winner of the English and Irish Derbys, was pitted against the best in Europe in the King George VI and Queen Elizabeth Diamond Stakes of 1975. The great French filly, Dahlia, who had already won this race in record time, was in the field. So was last year's St Leger winner, Bustino.

Bustino's connections intended him to win today. His two pacemakers, Highest and Kinglet, ensured that his was not to be a contest won merely by Grundy's turn of foot in the straight. This was to be a test of stamina and guts. Bustino had been tested in these departments, and not found wanting. Grundy was untried.

Bustino tracked his pacemakers. When Kinglet blew up and dropped out at the four-furlong marker, Joe Mercer pushed Bustino up into the lead. Lester Piggott on Dahlia, and Pat Eddery on Grundy, moved up into challenging position as they swung into the straight.

The question was never whether Bustino would falter. His strength was proven, his courage undoubted. Joe Mercer, too, was renowned as the strongest finisher in the business. The only question was whether the challengers had the brilliance to get close.

And brilliance it would take, for Bustino was two lengths ahead at the two-furlong post. Whips were out, and the gap had reduced to less than a length by the furlong marker. Dahlia, running a blinder, was left behind. Grundy was upsides his rival. The stands roared and rang. Bustino was weakening. Mercer, poised and vigorous as ever, thrust him on. Eddery urged on the chestnut with the flaxen mane and tail. The two horses touched. Bustino would not give up. Grundy would not withdraw his challenge . . .

Well, no wonder flat-racing is seldom a sport for poets. In the end, there can only be bathos: the simple sentence, "Grundy won." It did not seem thus to those of us who watched it, who roared ourselves hoarse urging one or the other, or – in my case, I think – both. There were tears. The stands rang to the echo. Everyone was aware that they had witnessed a duel not only between two brilliant horses, but between four relentless wills which had been tried to the ultimate and had still found more.

There are many great horses, but few truly great races. This was the greatest of them all.

The Gareth Edwards Try

The New Zealand rugby team that toured in 1973 had lacked that magical sprightliness and adventurousness which we have come to expect from the All Blacks. When they came to the end of the tour, however, nature could not be denied any longer. Their last match, against the Barbarians at Cardiff, started fast and furious. Bryan Williams, the All Black right-wing, ran with the ball to near the halfway line before deciding to kick. The ball fell beyond the Barbarian's 22, bounced and rolled towards the line. Phil Bennett raced back and retrieved it. He turned. He was on his own. A pack of heavyweight New Zealanders was bearing down on him.

Incredibly, Bennett did not kick for touch. He sidestepped four successive All Black tackles as the remainder of his team thundered back to help him. The great full-back, JPR Williams, was the first to reach him. Bennett passed to him. JPR was instantly tackled, and tackled high, but contrived to keep his footing and to pass to John Pullin, the English captain. By now there were three players lined up at Williams's left. Gareth Edwards, wrong-footed by the decision to run the ball from so close to the Barbarians's line, was still rushing back as the team began to move forward. He had to slam on the brakes and turn and run to catch up again.

Pullin passed out to John Dawes, who demonstrated his extraordinary skill with a dummy which took him past two challengers. He ran at a diagonal in order to reach his other backs. He passed out to Tom David at his right. David took the pass at the ten metre line. He did not feed on until he reached the halfway line.

The pass to Derek Quinnell was not a good one. Quinnell had to take the ball below knee-level. He looked to pass on to John Bevan, the Welsh wing, who had the speed and the pace to further the move.

The pass was a long one. It never reached its destination. Suddenly, Gareth Edwards, already travelling at maximum speed, burst through the line, intercepted the pass and ran for the corner-flag. The All Blacks were completely unprepared for the suddenness, the speed and the source of the threat. Only Grant Batty had a chance to catch Edwards on that last, 40 metre sprint. Batty flung himself at Edwards some three or four metres from the line, but Edwards was not there any more. He was airborne, diving for the line. Breaker after breaker of cheers crashed over him as he hit the turf again and pulled himself wearily to his feet, having scored what was surely the greatest try of modern times.

For once, it proved a scene-setter. None of the subsequent tries, of course, equalled this, but the game was a blinder, one of the most memorable battles on record. At the end, the Barbarians won 23–11.

The Great White Shark

This business of choosing the greatest ever is a surefire way of making enemies and attracting criticism. Like an England manager picking his team, for every one which I include, there will be three or four "but-what-abouts".

In selecting the 1993 British Open at Royal St George's as the greatest tournament in history, however, I hope to escape all accusations of unreasonable prejudice. The scorecards tell the story. Only one previous Open at Sandwich had been won with an under-par score. Yet 24 players finished below the regulation 280 in this phenomenal Championship.

This owed something, but not a lot, to the conditions. The heavens opened on the eve of the tournament after a dry spell which had rendered the course nigh unplayable. The course was refreshed. Greens were running. It owed something to the

weathermen, whose errors could have been predicted by you
and me, but not by the experts. The Birmingham Weather
Centre predicted hailstorms, blizzards and probably plagues
of locusts on the final day. Pin positions were adjusted accord-
ingly. The bad weather never came.

It owed more to the man who was to finish second in the
tournament. Over the past five years, Nick Faldo, the defending
champion, had established himself not merely as the foremost
golfer of his time but of all time. Faldo was so assiduous that he
faced accusations of being boring. He was the player who never
lost, who never cracked under pressure. His consistency was
unparalleled in the history of golf, and his single-mindedness
and dedication had, quite simply, lifted the quality of the whole
professional game. "He's not infallible. He can be beaten," said
Aussie Greg Norman before the beginning of the tournament. It
was a testament to Faldo that such a comment needed to be
made.

As for Norman, he was the nearly man. True, he had taken
the British Open back in 1986; but the Great White Shark, as he
was affectionately known, had a lamentable record of errors
and bad luck in major tournaments. In 1986, he led every major
going into the final round. He won the Open, but flunked the
rest. In the Masters, he needed a par at the last to tie with Jack
Nicklaus. He took five. In the USPGA of the same year, he led
by three shots with only seven holes to play. Bob Tway
famously holed from a bunker on the 18th to beat him. The
following year, in a play-off for the Masters, he was similarly
beaten by an outrageous chip-in by Larry Mize. Then came the
'88 Masters. Again, Norman merely needed a par at the
eighteenth to tie with Sandy Lyle, but played a half-hearted
medium iron shot and took five. In 1989, he shot a stunning 64
to get into the play-off of the British Open. He was on killing
form. He began the play-off with two birdies. He finished it
with an eighteenth from an amateur's nightmare, hacking
down the fairway with so many shots that he never even
completed the course. In 1990, it was Robert Gamez's turn
to hole a 7-iron second shot at the eighteenth to steal victory
from Norman in the Bay Hill tournament. That same year, in
the British Open, Norman received a brutal lesson in discipline
and course management from Nick Faldo in the third round at
St Andrews. The lesson appeared to be the oldest and cruellest:
your day is done. The new boys are in town, and they're ten
times more professional and dedicated than you and your

generation ever were. Move over. Reach for the zimmer frame. Fade.

Greg Norman faded. In the '93 Masters, he narrowly scraped the cut. In the '93 US Open, he didn't even make it.

When Norman set off on the first hole of the British Open, drove into heavy rough, took an 8-iron out, played two sand-wedges and double putted for a double bogey, no one was surprised. The rest of the round, however, was characteristic old-style Norman – brilliant, risky, unpredictable – but somehow it all panned out. Incredibly, an ebullient Norman was scrawling 66 on his scorecard on his return to the clubhouse. Faldo turned in a 69 and Bernhard Langer a 67, but Norman, Peter Senior and Americans Fuzzy Zoeller and Mark Calcavecchia shared the lead.

In perfect conditions the following morning, Langer set the standards for the rest of the competitors. He set them high, with a 66 which left him seven under par for the tournament. Fred Couples followed him in, just one shot behind. Nick Faldo, setting off on one under, had to shoot a comparable round if he was to stay in the hunt. His 5-iron approach to the first green finished just four feet from the pin. It was a declaration of intent. Faldo was to score eight threes and seven birdies in this blistering round, becoming in the process the first man ever to score 63 in an Open at Sandwich. Norman stayed in touch with a 68. Symbolically, it seemed, on this day when centuries-old records were tumbling, Jack Nicklaus, Tom Watson and Sandy Lyle failed to make the cut and gracefully took their leave. Ryder Cup player Colin Montgomerie did so gracelessly.

Saturday proved the calm before the storm. Faldo shot a 70 which, thanks to his efforts yesterday, looked positively pedestrian, but was quite the reverse. Corey Pavin, a relative newcomer with the look of a survivor from the Village People, hit a 70 and moved alongside the champion. Langer too shot 70. He would play with Norman (69). The USPGA laureate, Nick Price, scored 67, and moved into contention at five under.

Sunday dawned bright. The weather forecast said, "Yes, but wait until eleven o'clock. Those without sou'westers and arks will get caught flat-footed." We waited. Eleven o'clock came and went. Sunglasses remained the order of the day. Payne Stewart started the day's marvels by turning in a 63 to equal Faldo's record of two days ago. It was a fine round, but hardly comparable. Stewart was scratching around for a place down the field. Faldo had sunk every putt with the world watching him. Iain Pyman, the Leeds amateur, recorded a 71, giving him a total of 281, the best ever by an amateur in the Open.

Pyman won his deserved cheers, but the eyes of those who watched him on the eighteenth flickered constantly towards the electronic leader board, which told of heroic deeds out there in the country.

There are times in sport when men appear to defy the gods and when, extraordinarily, the gods suffer themselves to be defied – smile, even, upon a mere mortal's presumption. Gamblers refer to it as being "on a roll". Greg Norman was on a roll today.

For a long time, we could not believe it. Behind him, after all, Faldo was playing faultless golf, and we knew Norman's record. He would slice the ball into heavy rough and take eight to get out. He would hook into the lake and insist on donning a frogsuit. It was far more likely that Faldo would hit three successive holes in one than it was that Norman would carry on as he started.

Norman carried on as he started. He started perfectly. He was to miss just two greens, on both occasions because of unfortunate bounces. Oh, it didn't all go smoothly. At the seventh, he drove sublimely, then played a 4-iron which rocketed impatiently towards the flag, bounced and suddenly skittered off the green and down the slope. Norman putted, and the ball all but rolled back to his feet. The fatalists moaned. Norman holed out. At the next, with a 9-iron from 120 yards, he left the ball just 6 inches from the pin . . . and so it went on . . . and on . . .

Norman's were not the only prodigies performed that day. Faldo drove to the flag at the eleventh, hit it and holed the birdie putt. Langer had two birdies in a row, made his only mistake of the day when he took a driver at the fourteenth for the first time in the week, took a seven – destroying his chances of winning – but hit two more successive birdies.

It was between Norman and Faldo, then – between golf as unerring as the world has ever seen and golf touched, today, by genius. Faldo hit four birdies that day, Langer and Norman seven. At the par-four seventeenth, Norman at last showed signs of his previously all too evident humanity. "That was the first time I looked at the leader board," he was to recall. "I thought I was ahead." It was confirmed. He looked down again at a 14 inch putt. And missed. "My stomach fell a bit, but in a way it was the best thing that happened. I got lackadaisical on it, and it acted like a kick up the backside. Then I stood on the eighteenth tee. I said to myself to just swing and trust myself."

He just swung, and he split the fairway. 200 yards now from home. He took a 4-iron. The ball landed 20 feet from the pin. It rolled to just inside 15 feet of the dream. Even now there were those who thought that it might all yet go wrong, but most of us were convinced. We were witnessing something akin to a miracle that day. Most such phenomena are over in seconds. This one had been sustained for seventy-two holes and four extraordinary days.

The miracle happened.

Faldo rounded off a five-under-par 67 with a 10 foot putt to finish with what, in every rule-book, should have been an unbeatable 269. Norman emerged from the clubhouse to hug his wife. Others were there to congratulate him too. Bernhard Langer, who had finished on 270, shook his head in bemusement. He announced to Norman, "You've just played the greatest round of golf that I've ever seen." Gene Sarazen, 60 years after he had won the tournament, was incredulous: "This is the greatest Championship that I have ever seen. I've never witnessed such shots." Nick Faldo, from whom a "pretty fair" would sum up, say, Gene Kelly dancing on a pinhead, was almost effusive: "I'm not too disappointed (Trans: I'm gutted). I made a pretty good stab at defending my title (Trans: I broke my own record but I *could have done better*), but Greg just had a great day (Trans: Greg had a great day. What's the matter with me?). He was always that little bit too far ahead (Trans: I shall now go off and play the course six times just to see where I went wrong)."

But Faldo had done nothing wrong. That was the extraordinary nature of Norman's achievement. He had beaten the world's greatest golfer playing one of the world's greatest tournaments better than anyone had ever played it before. "Shark Devours Sandwich" ran the banner headline to a golfball advertisement a few days later. No one was arguing.

For what it is worth, this is what Norman achieved on those days when he was touched by stardust:

1. He played the best final round ever to win the Open.
2. He played the best first round ever by a Champion.
3. He recorded the lowest ever aggregate winning score on one of the world's most formidable links, incidentally shattering that course's records.
4. He beat the two best players in the world when they were on peak form, in what became a three-way matchplay.

So much for the nearly man.

Norman's own summary? "I hit every drive perfect, every iron perfect and I screwed up on only one little putt. I am in awe of just how well I played today."

No one accused him of arrogance. He was not claiming the achievement for himself. He was rightly in awe. So were we all.

The Real All-Rounders

C. B. Fry captained England at cricket as one of the great batsmen of all time and a good fast bowler. He held the world long-jump record. He played football for England and appeared in an FA Cup Final. He only failed to win a rugby blue because of injury. All this, and he only had one lung! When, in retirement, he mentioned to a friend in his club that he would now interest himself in horseracing, attach himself to a stable and then set up on his own, the friend asked: "What as, Charles? Trainer, horse or jockey?"

Denis Compton, another cavalier batting genius who, of course, played for Middlesex and England, spent his winters playing for Arsenal and England. In his first game of rugby, he scored most of the tries and kicked all the goals. His partner at Middlesex, Bill Edrich, played for Tottenham Hotspur. Both men were left-wingers.

England captain Brian Close had been centre-forward for Arsenal and Leeds. England's 1966 World Cup hero, Geoff Hurst, played for Essex, while his West Ham colleague, Jim Standen, was a regular with Worcestershire. Both were in the winning FA Cup team of 1964. Ian Botham, of course, took the field for Scunthorpe United, whilst his friend, colleague and sparring partner, Viv Richards, played for Antigua in the qualifying tournament for the 1978 World Cup. Andy Ducat spent his entire working life on a playing field – and ended it there. In winter, he played for Arsenal, Aston Villa, Fulham and England; in summer, he played for Surrey and England. He maintained both jobs from 1906 to 1924. He died whilst batting at Lord's.

Gerry McElhinney of Bolton Wanderers had been a double international at boxing and Gaelic football. Jackie Coulter, who played 11 times for Northern Ireland at soccer, had been roller-skating champion of all Ireland!